ESSENTIAL NEGOTIATION SKILLS FOR RECRUITERS

ESSENTIAL NEGOTIATION SKILLS FOR RECRUITERS

TWELVE GOLDEN RULES TO TRANSFORM YOUR NEGOTIATING SUCCESS AND YOUR INCOME

DAVID McCLEMENTS

Maclemons International Ltd

First published in Great Britain as a softback original in 2021
Copyright © David McClements

The moral right of this author has been asserted.

Typeset in Charter

Editing, design, typesetting and publishing by UK Book Publishing
www.ukbookpublishing.com

ISBN: 978-1-913179-79-3

For my wonderful Family

"*Let us never negotiate out of fear,*
but let us never fear to negotiate"

—————————————

JOHN F KENNEDY,
FORMER PRESIDENT
OF THE UNITED STATES

TABLE OF CONTENTS

ABOUT THE AUTHOR

David McClements (or "Mac Lemons" as many people know him!) is an international speaker and trainer who has literally circumnavigated the globe helping businesses and organizations in his key areas of expertise – Sales, Negotiation, and People Management and Motivation.

After starting his career in Procter & Gamble UK in sales, he went into the world of consultancy, training prominent sales forces in the UK and Ireland before starting his own consulting business in 1999 Whitewater International Training & Consultancy. (Now named Maclemons International – www.maclemons.com)

Having travelled far and wide, David developed his skills with world-famous business and personal development experts such as Richard Bandler, Paul McKenna, Anthony Robbins, Jay Abraham, Al Gore, John Gray, Dan Poynter and many others. Whitewater soon became well-known experts in blending the skills and techniques of personal development with key business skills, matched with engaging, informal methods of delivery, and maybe even a little comedy

thrown in! This unique blend quickly established the business as one of the most influential training and development organizations in the UK and has gone on to have a truly global client list.

Following the development of his "Twelve Golden Rules of Negotiation", David has trained thousands of people in the recruitment industry across the world, helping his clients gain staggering results in a very short space of time. As a result of that work this book is born.

David is also a motivational speaker, delivering keynote speeches at many conferences for some of the world's biggest brands across the globe, incorporating his own personal unique style of heartwarming and passionate delivery.

A multi qualified NLP professional, David is also an Advanced qualified driver and motorcycle rider, as well as qualified Scuba diver. His passions are Rugby and Motorcycling.

ACKNOWLEDGEMENTS

I have not attempted to cite in the text all the authorities and sources consulted in the preparation of this manual. To do so would require more space than is available. The list would include departments of various governments, libraries, industrial institutions, periodicals and many individuals.

I do though have to say thank you to all the delegates over the years who have contributed so much to my own knowledge of these skills. You have taught me a lot.

Thanks also to Gill Branthwaite for her painstaking translation of my writings. Thanks also to Romney Rawes, the legend of the recruitment industry for his feedback and guidance, Crawfurd Walker of R.I.B (Recruitment Industry Benchmarking) as well as Denise Walker for their invaluable input and experience.

WHAT YOU NEED TO KNOW FIRST

Hello and thank you for reading.

What do the years 2009 and 2020 have in common? They have been economic game changers! Throw out the rule book and start thinking differently events. When these huge economic shifts occur, the recruitment industry is one which really feels it!

Did you ever imagine a situation where the entire country was told to stay at home? Covid-19 has changed the world in ways we have yet to see and has had economic consequences which will take years to fully come to light. Many businesses will not make it to the far end and for those that do, there will be incredible financial pressures upon them which will mean serious examination of staff numbers and in turn recruitment.

The recruiters themselves who survive have to get better. And they will certainly have to be better negotiators. Let me give some more background.

After more than 10 years of unprecedented economic stability in the UK up to 2009, business in general was booming, people were hiring and the marketplace for recruitment was buoyant. In such times the climate was right for real growth in recruitment, both in the number of placements and the number of recruitment businesses.

This in itself created challenges. If there was lots of work, and many new recruiters could appear, most often the competitive strategy they would adopt would be one simply based on price and under-cutting competition. Immediately the industry was under considerable margin pressure even though the number of roles available to fill was massive. A person in their back bedroom saying they could do work at ridiculously low rates vs. medium sized companies grafting away to compete against them, and massive organisations needing to keep pricing and margins up to sustain such large operations. Simultaneously there had been the growth of the internet and job sites etc. All recruitment businesses felt these effects keenly, but some of those larger recruitment businesses, in my view, committed margin suicide. This was a "race to the bottom".

Everything was changing for recruitment. It was a new world in which old business models no longer applied – and the knee-jerk reaction was to drop prices. What should they have done? And what did the ones that I worked with do? They learned how to sell and negotiate better.

Then came the global economic collapse in 2008. Hiring freezes, with companies battening down the hatches to try to ride out the storm, squeezing every last penny out of their finances. And the result for recruitment? Many, many recruiters, fighting for fewer and fewer placements and another massive pressure on pricing and margin. This pattern has been evident through all recessionary periods over the past 40 years.

In addition, the growth and expansion of the technology available to run recruitment was exponential and meant many individuals and organisations saw the need for classic recruiters as obsolete.

Fast forward to 2020. Entire countries ground to a complete halt. The exact same things as described above will happen again, if not substantially worse. It is so sad to say but in 2021 there are going to be many people out of work and looking for fewer and fewer jobs. One interesting dynamic though with the 2020 crisis is that companies in general are going to find out they CAN actually work substantially differently. They may have been faced with their entire workforce having to work from home and be managed remotely and therefore try to automate or go online as much as possible. That means there will be even MORE technology available to replace recruiters! So, what do you do?

> **One thing is for sure – from now you are not going to get what you deserve. You are going to get what you can negotiate!**

Here are a few thoughts on the recruitment industry as a whole.

The recruitment industry has little to no barriers to entry. Anyone can start a recruitment business: 1 or 2 person outfits up to global multinationals. There have been many poor role models! Fly-by-night businesses, as well as individuals within larger organisations, more concerned about their fee or their bonus than either the needs of the client or the candidate.

Historically, the recruitment industry has not necessarily had a great reputation. You may have, even your business may have, but the industry hasn't. Traffic wardens, car sales people, bankers and the tax man could easily be lumped in with recruiters in the "disliked" category with the notion being recruiters are merely "human estate agents"!

However, it is my view that much of the blame for the bad reputation rests with the industry itself. In general, the wider world has no idea what good recruitment professionals actually do and how hard they work – the problem is they think they know! Recruiters don't talk enough about the full extent of the service they offer, the actual effort put in, and why it is worth paying for.

If someone believes you sift CVs for a living, throw lots of them at a client and see what sticks, why would they want to pay a lot of money for a basic service like that?

Many recruiters have been taught "tricks of the trade", but not how to really sell well – stand up for their fees – or negotiate their position successfully. Those who have made the crucial investment in this type of learning have also not ensured it becomes "how we do things here". A number of owner managers I have worked with refuse to ensure there are proper controls and support in place to protect both the recruiter and the business. Why? Because they do not like process! No matter how skilled an individual recruiter is, without the right environment, he/she will be under pressure to sell at any cost and work on rubbish business.

It is my view that due to this lack of ability to negotiate properly the industry as a whole has simply, time and again, gone for reduced fees and margin, and has effectively pressed the accelerator in that race to the bottom. This damages and undermines the entire industry and recruiters still have to do the same work for a lot less money, or worse, even more work for less money.

However, one good thing for the industry is that often in these economic game changing moments many fly-by-night businesses and individuals are pushed out, somewhat cleansing the system.

I have to say, though, I have met countless recruiters who meet every single candidate they have, genuinely understand their skills and potential, and work incredibly hard to find roles to suit them, having simultaneously been truly committed to understanding the requirements of the client. Early morning interviews are the norm, as well as those going on into the evening to help the worlds of all concerned.

Sadly, there will still be those who have little to no business experience themselves, seem to make a point of deriding clients and their processes, don't meet their candidates, are genuinely not that concerned about what they are doing, and purely engage in transactional activity for the fee. There will always be people like this in any industry, and the aspiration for all should be to prove them wrong and become the model of change you want to see.

If you are an honest, hardworking recruitment professional, genuinely concerned with building the careers of your candidates and the businesses of your clients, you will get a lot from this book.

You are about to learn how to earn more for the work you do and, amazingly, even how to do the same work for the same fees and still go on to earn more.

> Let's be absolutely clear from the outset: taking your fee down until the other party says yes is <u>not</u> negotiating – that is <u>discounting</u> and requires little skill or intelligence.

The difference between the two will be fully explained in due course. Unfortunately, it is the route many in recruitment have chosen. A belief that "Price is King", and the only option is to reduce fees, is the basis for failure. The purpose of this book is to illustrate why that is not necessarily the case and what to do differently. If price was the only thing people cared about, Brands could not exist.

How this book came to be

Many moons ago I was asked by a client if I did any training on negotiation skills, to which I automatically replied yes. In all honesty, I really thought I knew about negotiation and that I was good at it. Unfortunately, the more I read and came to understand about the topic, the clearer it became that I knew nothing and I was a fool! Not being very good at something is bad, but not knowing how rubbish you really are, is worse.

The more I learned, the more I came to understand that easily applied principles seemed to be the crux of the matter, and out of this were born the 12 Golden Rules: Simple, easy steps which cause a shift in mindset, a subsequent transformation of skillset and ultimately better results.

I am convinced these principles work. I have put them into practice personally, trained thousands of people upon them, and they themselves have had staggering results. I know because they have told me. Story after story after story. Clients, by investing in these negotiation skills, have put tens of millions on the bottom line. They showed me the numbers. You can do the same.

Finally, I appreciate there are many different types of recruitment services which need different approaches (e.g. from high volume/low margin industrial, to high end search and selection) but that quality mindset still needs to be applied in any form of recruitment to earn proper fees. Hence this book.

How the Book Works

I will use countless examples throughout the book for which I make no apology. I have found they are the best way of illustrating the principles, making them easily understood and appreciated, and more importantly, easily applied. It is often the case that years later I meet former attendees of the training programme and it is the examples which have stuck with them. All the examples in the chapters are in a shaded area for ease of reference.

Often these examples will include exact words used in the conversations and this is deliberate for two reasons:

1. It makes the explanation easier
2. It is the exact words people use in negotiation which matter and the examples highlight this.

In addition, percentages seem to be the language of the recruitment industry, with rates being quoted as a percentage fee. So, in many of the examples I will use percentages for ease of understanding, but in Golden Rule 4 you will find out why percentages can be the wrong thing to talk about!

There is also repetition of key messages throughout. Things which seem to crop up over and over again, and this is for a reason – they matter!

There are also overlaps between the Golden Rules. By their nature the principles interlink, overlap and intertwine, and are fundamentally connected to each other, so often within a chapter you may be referred to another Golden Rule to further explain. This is unavoidable and helps show how the Golden Rules help each other to form the powerful skillset they can provide.

A key premise to understand from the start is that you negotiate "with" people not "against" people. The purpose of negotiation is to find a way with which both parties are happy and this is done "with" and not "against" them. In chapter 1 we only ever refer to the "other party" in a negotiation, not the "other side". Sides infer win/lose situations; other parties infer finding a mutually beneficial outcome.

To finish, the purpose of this book is to help worthy professionals perform a worthy job, for a worthy fee. Read on, discover how, and enjoy a life of more abundance.

WARNING—DISCLAIMER

The publisher and author are not engaged in rendering legal, accounting or other professional services. If legal or other expert assistance is required, the services of a competent professional should be sought.

It is not the purpose of this book to reprint all the information that is otherwise available to authors and/or publishers, but instead to complement, amplify and supplement other texts. You are urged to read all the available material, learn as much as possible and tailor the information to your individual needs.

Every effort has been made to make this publication as complete and as accurate as possible. However, there *may be mistakes*, both typographical and in content. Therefore, this text should be used only as a general guide and not as the ultimate source of information. Furthermore, this manual contains information that is current only up to the printing date.

The purpose of this manual is to educate and entertain. The author and publisher shall have neither liability nor responsibility to any person or entity with respect to any loss or damage caused, or alleged to have been caused, directly or indirectly, by the information contained in this book.

If you do not wish to be bound by the above, you may return this book to the publisher for a full refund.

CHAPTER ONE

GOLDEN RULE NO. 1

"Stop negotiating and sell better"

"If you believe you always have to negotiate,
you always will."

———

AUTHOR

It might seem strange to be told the first step of good negotiation is not to negotiate! I was quite surprised by this discovery myself, but hopefully by the end of this chapter alone it will be apparent why this has to be Golden Rule No. 1.

The first question I ask every delegate on the 12 Golden Rules training programme is very simple . . .

"What is the difference between selling and negotiating?" If you go on a Selling Skills training course, and a Negotiation Skills training course, what is the difference?

Take some time to consider what your answer is. Really think about it – it's important. What do you think the difference between selling and negotiating is?

99.9% of the time I receive the following answers:

1. There is no difference between the two; or,
2. Selling is one-way and one-sided, whereas negotiation is two-way and collaborative; or,
3. Negotiation is *part* of the sales process.
4. Selling is getting someone interested in a product or service and negotiating is finding a mutually agreeable price, or terms.

Well here is the news:

1. There is a big difference between the two.
2. Good selling is not one-way at all.
3. Negotiation is not part of the sales process. There is a point where selling stops and negotiation starts and great sellers don't have to negotiate.

We are going to use the diagram below over and over again in this book. It will be the main method of showing the rules and how they work.

Below is our spectrum:

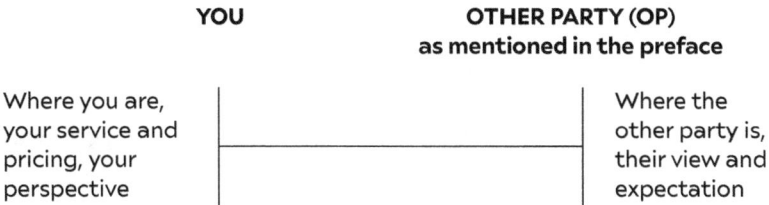

YOU	OTHER PARTY (OP)
	as mentioned in the preface
Where you are, your service and pricing, your perspective	Where the other party is, their view and expectation

Selling is bringing the other party to you, to where they agree on your product and price.

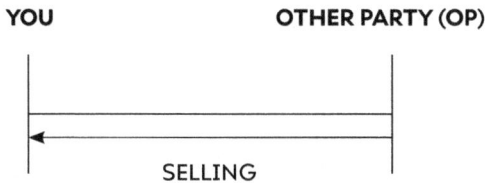

YOU   OTHER PARTY (OP)

SELLING

Negotiating is when you leave your starting point, pricing, or service, and move towards the other party, and it usually costs! Once you start changing terms or pricing, selling stops and negotiating starts.

This is absolutely fundamental to understand. There is a specific point at which you have stopped selling and have started the skill set of negotiation. This book of course focusses on the negotiation part.

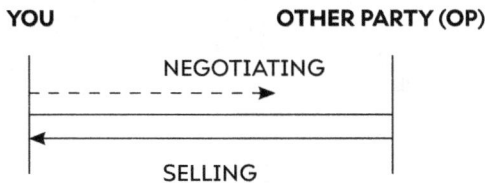

YOU   OTHER PARTY (OP)

NEGOTIATING

SELLING

So, I often ask the question, "Is it possible for the other party to come all the way over to you and be happy?" To my astonishment many people say No! Why on earth not? If you have what they want or need, and can show options they didn't even think they could have, it is entirely possible.

It happens to you as a buyer all the time. You buy something for the price asked and you are happy to do so.

Where has the attitude which sees "selling" as undesirable, one-way and un-collaborative come from? Why do we think that selling is talking people into things they don't want, for prices they don't want to pay, and only in the interest of the seller?

Think of the first three words which come into your mind when I say "salesman".

The replies I receive are usually:

1. Dodgy
2. Cheap suit
3. Untrustworthy

. . . Slimy, and many other quite unflattering words!

Now think of three industries that come to mind when I say "salesman".

Again, the normal replies involve:

1. Cars
2. Double glazing
3. Estate agents

. . . Insurance and a few others.

(NB – I deliberately used the word "salesman" and not "salesperson" or any other word. From experience when I use "salesman" it engenders a more negative response than any other – which is what we are after.)

So, are these words and phrases positive images? Not at all. Selling has been hijacked!

The concept of sales in the UK has been hijacked by industries which have proven to be every bit as untrustworthy as they are perceived. As such, "Sales" has become a dirty word and the perception of it tarnished in the minds of us all, seen as a one-way, win/lose interaction. This is an absolute tragedy.

In fact, in the UK and Ireland we now have a pathological fear of sales people where even in adverts on the radio and television it is specifically mentioned that "no sales person will call"!

The paranoia regarding sales runs even further, to the extent that often sales people no longer even exist within organisations! – they are all now "Customer Business Development Executives", "Account Managers", "Account Directors" or "Business Development Managers" or "Strategic Account Managers"! The list goes on.

Real selling is not how we have come to perceive it at all. Real selling is a two-way process involving a genuine understanding of what the customer really needs (Customer Needs Analysis – CNA) and then showing how the product or service an individual has can meet that need, and why it is worth the price being asked. What exactly is wrong with that? Is a customer gaining what they need really so bad?

If you bought something, somebody sold it. The pen you use every day, somebody sold it. The chair you are sitting on, somebody sold it. Does that make them a bad person? Of course it doesn't.

The fact is that EVERYONE is in sales! If you are providing a service to a client and talk to the client about it, you are in sales.

Ever been on a date? (And my sincerest wish here is that you have!) Before the date did you take a little longer to get ready? Spend a bit more time choosing clothes? Engage in topics of conversation you usually wouldn't whilst you were out? Why?

Because you want the other person to "buy" you. We are all in sales: get used to it.

One of my earliest business heroes, Sir John Harvey Jones, the former Chairman of ICI and host of the first few series of the BBC programme "Troubleshooter", famously said,

"Selling is the transfer of benefit".

Real selling involves helping people see the opportunities to have their needs met and meeting them.

Have you ever gone into a shop, spent more money than you wanted to, and been happy? Most people readily admit – yes! But how is that possible? How is it even conceivable that you spend more money than you wanted to and yet be happy?

Mostly the replies I receive are very simple:

1. I got what I wanted.
2. I felt like I got a bargain.
3. I realised there were things I could buy or options I could have I was unaware of.
4. I was really "helped" by the person I was engaging with (i.e. they were sold to!).

So, is that such a bad thing? Do you think the "sales person" who "helped" you is a terrible individual indulging in a one-way sales process to your detriment?

Real selling, this two-way process outlined above, brings the other party to you and it is eminently possible for them to be happy about it. Recruiters need to learn how to do this better. They need to be able to elegantly, powerfully and persuasively show their value and expertise.

Let me give you a real life personal example of selling to illustrate my point.

The New Suit

EXAMPLE

I used to live in Woking, Surrey. I had just moved there and was out exploring the town on a Saturday around 5:25pm. On my wander I saw a really nice store which had what appeared to be men's and women's clothing of high quality and looked inviting.

I hate shopping! Trying stuff on in busy stores and all the messing about involved truly puts me off, so I try to avoid shopping as much as I can.

However, at that time I did need a new suit, so I tentatively entered the store to have a look, safe in the knowledge, at 5:25pm, it was probably closing time, and my perceived ordeal was unlikely to happen.

As I walked in, a very pleasant guy with an Italian accent greeted me and asked if he could help, to which I gave the standard answer that I was only looking around. I was assured that was no problem at all and to feel free.

Because most of my attention was placed on going through the suits, the guy quietly approached and asked if it was suits I was most interested in. I said yes and he asked me why.

"Oh, I think I need a new one for work."

"Really, okay. What sort of work do you do?"

I told him I ran training programmes all over the world and just needed something which looked really smart. However, I also highlighted it was now 5:30pm and he was probably closing so not to worry too much.

"We are open until 7 o'clock, sir, so don't worry about that. Would you like a coffee?"

Somewhat surprised, but pleasantly, I thought at least I was going to get a free cup of coffee!

"What colour suit were you thinking of, sir?"

"Blue."

"Single or double breasted?"

"Double, I think."

"I wouldn't, sir. Double breasted is not really in fashion. You are a size 40, right?"

I hadn't been measured or tried anything on yet! He just knew. He took three suits off the rack, suggested they might be appropriate, and encouraged me to try them on. I put on the first one, came out of the changing room, and we both instantaneously hated it! It didn't look right at all. Out I came in the second (the most expensive) and I have to say – I liked it. He, however, didn't!

"It just doesn't suit your shape, sir. The cut is wrong for your build and just doesn't look right. I wouldn't want you to buy it!" He then proceeded to show me why the cut of it didn't work and I could see it for myself.

Out I came in the third option and it just felt right. As soon as it was on I knew I liked it and so did he!

The guy then brought me a shirt, still in its packet and said, "*Now try that on.*"

"Oh don't worry about it. Don't open a packet on my account; you'll only have to fold it up again."

"*Folding it up is my job, sir.*"

So, I was back in the changing room, putting the shirt on, when all of a sudden a tie was flicked over the top of the changing cubicle. "*Try that on too, sir.*"

I dutifully put the whole lot on and walked out – I felt like James Bond! It all looked fantastic.

"*Shoes!*" he exclaimed, guessing my size correctly. I put them on.

He was immediately down on the floor, pinning the trousers to the right length and at the end stood up and said, "*What do you think?*"

Truth is – I loved it and I bought it – all of it – suit, shirt, tie, and shoes – the lot!

I had absolutely no intention of buying a suit that day, never mind spending that amount of money but I left elated. Why?

1. I got what I felt really worked for me.
2. I **felt** good (more of that in Golden Rule No. 3).
3. I was evidently dealing with a professional. An expert who knew what he was talking about and amply demonstrated that.

P.S. Here's the slightly embarrassing part. I went back the following Saturday purely to pick up the trousers which had needed to be adjusted, and he again talked me into more clothes. I still loved it!

What is that supposed to illustrate? Several things:

1. People like people who solve their problems.
2. People like to deal with people who are professional and expert and are easy to deal with.
3. Real selling is a two-way interactive process which brings the other party to you by showing how their needs are being met.
4. When the above is done well, negotiation is nowhere to be seen because it is not necessary.

I have been approached many, many times by organisations who tell me their sales force (if that's what they still call it!) needs better negotiation skills. As a matter of course, I always spend time with the sales force to see what the current circumstances are and what they do in those circumstances. 99% of the time I discover the same thing – they don't need better negotiation skills; they need better selling skills.

The sales person shows their product or service, usually in a way that is unpersuasive and showing no real advantages to buying it.

The buyer then unleashes the Black Belt of all negotiation skills for which they have evidently been in years of preparation. They are met with a firm No!

Almost immediately, the sales person reaches for their calculator and starts working out how they can make the product cheaper and "do them a deal". They start heading straight over to the other party, and that's why the business and the individuals concerned are convinced they need enhanced negotiation skills to do this better.

SALES PERSON   **OTHER PARTY (OP)**

BRING THE OP TO YOU

STAY HERE, SELL BETTER

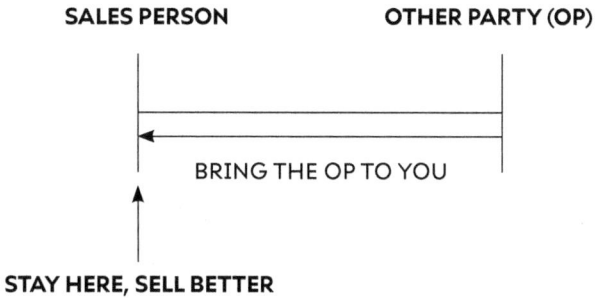

What they really need is better selling skills to enable them to stay where they are:

- Better customer needs analysis.
- Better presentations and ways of showing the value of their product or service.
- Better objection handling techniques to answer the most common queries.
- Better closing capabilities.

If they had these, the chances are they would end up in far fewer negotiations!

It is the same for you as a worthy recruiter. You have to stand your ground and be eloquent in showing what you do for your clients, and why, in the famous words of L'Oreal, "You're worth it"!

If you don't do this, you will simply be put in the same class as many of your unworthy competitors. Undeserving of decent fees, and relentlessly beaten up by clients on price.

Is there any professional judgment in what you do? Is there any skill involved in understanding client needs, matching them to candidates, and working the process seamlessly for both?

If your answer is 'not really, we all mostly have the same candidates and it is a commodity we have to sell like a tin of beans', join the masses and simply take your fees down as it is the only way you will succeed.

If your answer is 'yes', then for goodness sake stand up for yourself and your profession. Actively show, and talk clients through all of the work you will do for them. Show what's involved; illustrate why dealing with you is better than the next person and *prove* you are worth it.

If you do indeed have the same candidates as your competitors, the only real difference for the client is YOU.

The candidate is not the product in recruitment – you are.

CHAPTER SUMMARY

1. There is a difference between selling and negotiation.

2. There is a point where one stops and the other starts.

3. People like to deal with experts and professionals who evidently know what they are doing. Be that professional, knowledgeable, expert.

4. Good sellers negotiate less because they don't have to.

5. The only person capable of showing the other party the value of yourself and your service is you.

6. If you believe you have to negotiate – you will always negotiate.

Stop Negotiating – Sell Better.

So, when selling has stopped, let's look at how to negotiate.

CHAPTER TWO

GOLDEN RULE NO· 2

"It's about belief systems and comfort levels"

"In business you don't get what you deserve, you get what you negotiate"

DR CHESTER L KARRASS

So based on the assumption that all selling has failed and you now have to move into the world of negotiation, let's get straight into what it's all about and exactly how to do it.

What both parties believe is possible, and how comfortable they are with the negotiation process, drives all negotiation.

The western world, and particularly the UK and Ireland, in many ways is a retailer's heaven. In general, we go into a shop, ask how much something is, and pay the price. Fixed price, no negotiation. It is a pure buy/sell transaction.

Not only that, but we are also culturally bound in such a way that we see even *trying* to negotiate or asking for a discount as embarrassing!

You must have experienced the type of situation where in a shop someone starts to ask for "a deal" on a purchase, and you can see the evident discomfort of the person accompanying them. "Can you give me anything off?" says the person, and their friend or relative immediately nudges them to say "stop it"! The staff member replies that they do not have the authority to give a discount so the person says, "Okay, can I talk to the manager then?" "Stop it! This is embarrassing. Stop it! I'm going to wait in Starbucks!"

Here is the really strange part. That same embarrassed person who found it all intolerable in the shop, flies on holiday to Turkey and instantaneously upon arrival changes into Del Boy – the famous wheeler dealer from the eternally popular BBC comedy programme *Only Fools and Horses*.

That same person is now thoroughly willing to haggle, for protracted lengths of time, over small amounts of money, on items they probably don't even want that much. What has happened? Unless they have been watching Negotiation Skills videos on the flight over, something has changed.

What has changed is what the person believes is acceptable and achievable. What has changed are their belief systems and comfort levels. They now believe it is acceptable to haggle and so feel comfortable doing it. Amazingly, when they return to the UK, they immediately revert to their old embarrassed self.

I have asked thousands of people on my programme, "Who here haggles?" Usually half of each of the groups in the UK raises their hands.

"What do you haggle on?"

"Cars, houses, white goods, electrical goods."

"Why?"

"Because you can," is often the reply.

"Okay then, do you negotiate on clothes, for example?" Most people say no.

"Why not?"

"Because you can't!"

Well, you can, especially if you are buying multiple items, or spending quite a lot of money. (I have many stories from delegates who, following the programme, went out and successfully did it for themselves.)

"Well I would if it's faulty," I am often answered.

"Well why don't you ask even if it isn't?"

"Because you can't" is what I hear over and over again.

Belief = you can't! Comfort level = very low.

The truth is, most stores really do have the ability to offer discounts, often 10%, and there most definitely is a facility at the tills to allow that discount to happen! Just ask anyone who has worked in retail.

You see, the examples above perfectly illustrate the point of belief systems and comfort levels. You certainly can haggle on cars, houses, white goods and electrical goods, but also clothes and indeed practically anything. Mobile phone contracts, insurance renewals, mortgages, cable or satellite packages, landlines, internet, holidays, hotels, furniture, carpets . . .

Furthermore the ability to do this has grown massively post 2009. With the economic collapse, and normal folk struggling so much for money, every business has had to focus on getting every sale they can. The internet has also made a huge change to how people shop. As such, the ability of everyone to price hunt and price compare has grown exponentially. 2020, and all Covid 19 has brought to bear, means this will be even more enormous. With this comes the ability to negotiate if you have done a little homework (yes, even in the major outlets), but many people don't even try to do that! Why? Embarrassment (discomfort).

So, there are often three categories of people:

1. Those who never ask (either because they believe they can't or feel very uncomfortable doing it).
2. Those who would only ask in particular industry sectors or circumstances.
3. Those who always ask, if not for money off, for something else thrown in.

The worst that can ever happen as a result of asking is a 'no'. Nobody dies and life goes on. The best is that you save money and/or get things for free!

So, as a buyer, always ask! If they can't give you money off, ask for something thrown in!

Now, it would be an insane assertion for me to say it will always work 100% of the time, because it won't. However, I can promise you if you never ask, you will get nothing, 100% of the time.

So how is all of the above relevant to the recruitment industry?

Like the general public, organisations are also now severely pressed for cash. Budgets are cut and there is close scrutiny of every penny of expenditure.

Using our Turkey holiday analogy again, do buyers of recruitment services in the UK believe they are shopping in the UK? Do they think you tell them what the price is and they pay it? Of course they don't.

They believe they are shopping in Turkey – everything is negotiable. Because they believe that, they are increasingly comfortable about asking for (or demanding) a reduction in fees. Furthermore, it's their job! People are paid to minimise costs and manage their budgets. If they aren't doing that they are being negligent in their role. It's their job to do so! It has nothing to do with you as a person, and all others in your line of work are being challenged by them in the same way.

That is why your own "Belief Systems and Comfort Levels" and those within the recruitment industry as a whole have to change.

I have witnessed recruiters sit back laughing disparagingly following a telephone call when the client didn't even ask for a reduction in fees, and then be absolutely panicked when other ones do.

"Help! Get me my manager, they are playing hard ball."

Believe and accept that being challenged hard on rates is going to happen – consistently – for the rest of your career and become comfortable dealing with it, either by selling better or, if you have to, negotiate using all the principles of this book.

Once you accept and anticipate you are going to be eternally challenged on pricing, see it is okay and normal, and become comfortable handling it, you really start to improve your own results and could potentially be part of the process of stopping that damn race to the bottom!

CHAPTER SUMMARY

1. Belief Systems and Comfort Levels drive negotiation.

2. You can negotiate on almost everything.

3. It is going to happen to you consistently for the rest of your career.

4. Get comfortable and learn how to deal with it.

CHAPTER THREE

GOLDEN RULE NO· 3

"A good deal is in your head!"

"In negotiation, we must find a solution that pleases everyone, because no-one accepts that they must lose and the other must win . . . Both must win"

NABIL N JAMAL

If recruiters are smart, they are not looking for a one-off transaction with a client, but rather want to cultivate an ongoing relationship within which all parties benefit, and further business will ensue.

Recruitment should never be seen as a one hit wonder such as a double glazing sales person whom you will never see in your life again. Even if it is just one role, in a small business, you never know what can become of that business, or who they know, and how your own business can grow.

As such, the key to any successful negotiation is both parties being happy with the outcome – often described as "win/win". If someone feels "beaten" they rarely want to feel it again, so they don't come back.

In my opinion one of the greatest business and personal development books ever written is Steven Covey's "The Seven Habits of Highly Successful People". If you haven't read it, I really recommend you do. He talks at length about the simple principle of win/win in his "Habit 4", highlighting three vital character traits of people and organisations who approach negotiation or potential conflict with a win/win attitude:

1. Integrity – sticking with your true feelings, values and commitments.
2. Maturity – expressing your ideas and feelings with courage and consideration for the ideas and feelings of others.
3. Abundance Mentality – believing there is plenty for everyone.

So using our simple diagram again:

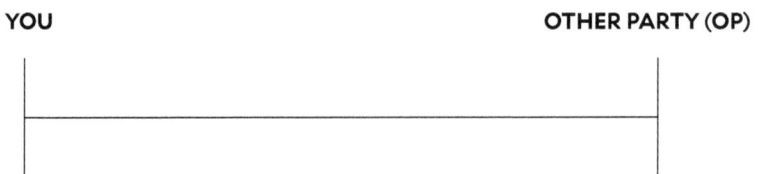

YOU   **OTHER PARTY (OP)**

I always ask delegates on the programme to identify where win/win is on the spectrum, and unfortunately most of the time I am given a worrying answer . . .

YOU   **OTHER PARTY (OP)**

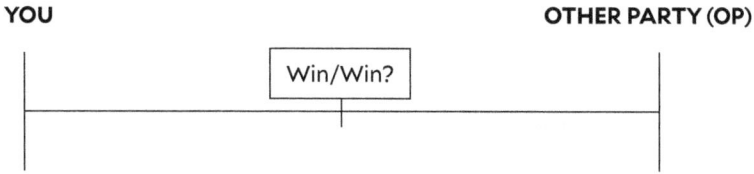

. . . it's in the middle!

Now, that is a worry! To be fair, if everyone knew where it really is, they probably wouldn't be on my training programme! It is natural to think everyone meeting halfway is win/win, but a skilled negotiator getting you to meet them halfway might be ripping you off!

Where is win/win really?

It is any place where both parties are happy with the outcome – and that can be anywhere on the spectrum . . .

YOU   **OTHER PARTY (OP)**

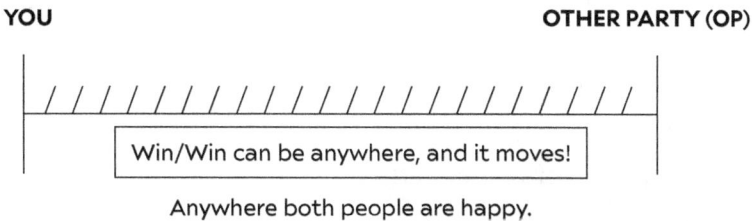

Anywhere both people are happy.

Let's look at a number of examples of win/win and how it moves around.

Take an example where you have the perfect answer to the client's problem – an exclusive candidate for example – they desperately need it and they pay full fee for it. That is the other party getting what they want; their problem is solved, they are happy and no doubt so are you.

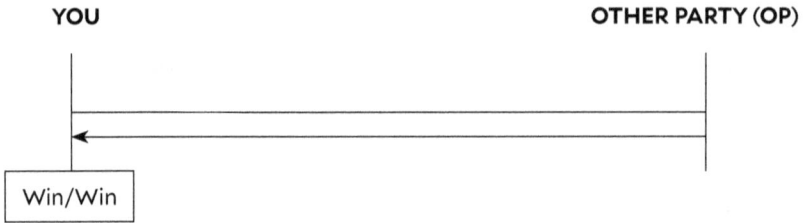

YOU   **OTHER PARTY (OP)**

Win/Win

At the start of a fiscal year, or the beginning of a billing period, you would often be more bullish and only want to, or be willing to, or be happy to, give a little from your position; only small changes in your fees, or the level of your service, because you have time to do more work and the pressure is less.

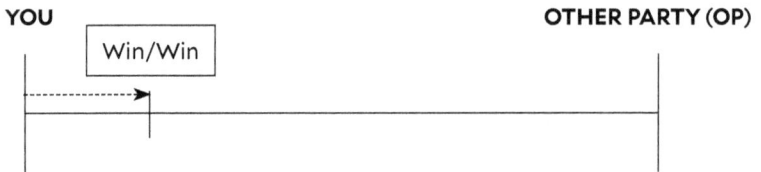

YOU   **OTHER PARTY (OP)**

Win/Win

Come the end of a fiscal or billing period, however, with pressure on you to get more numbers on the board, you might be willing to go a whole lot further – now the new position is win/win. I have known some recruiters who would practically place their own grandmother to hit their end of year target!

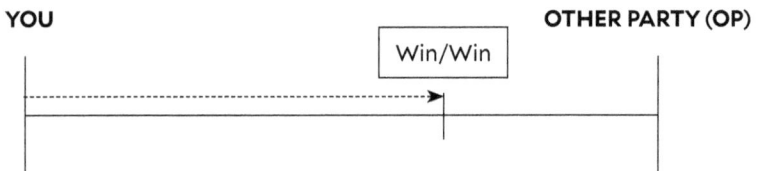

YOU   **OTHER PARTY (OP)**

Win/Win

You see, it's not where you end up, it's how you feel about where you end up (see also Golden Rule No. 7).

I can give lots of examples where even massive multi-national businesses have changing perspectives about what win/win looks like given the circumstances they are in, what targets they are ultimately chasing and the exact timing of the transactions. What appears to be a good deal is dependent on the circumstances at that time. What you see as okay and acceptable changes, given the circumstances.

I know for a fact that whoever you are reading this book, I can out-negotiate you! Bold statement, eh? However, I also know for a fact you can out-negotiate me! How can these two statements be true? Well, it simply depends on what we are negotiating about and when. How much I need what you have, and when we are talking about it.

The major point to realise is that a good deal *is a feeling* about where you end up, and not the end point in itself.

The iPad and Speakers

EXAMPLE

Imagine being on the programme upon which this book is based. I hold up an iPad and speakers which connect to it, and say, "someone make me an offer for these 2 items".

Usually there is some comedian in the audience who shouts, "£20" or even more of a derisory offer! I immediately walk towards them and say "Deal" and shake their hand.

I then ask them, "What is the first thing to enter your head right now?" to which they reply, *"Damn, I should have said less!"* Now they are disappointed. Yes, they got a deal, but they will be niggled by their own feeling of disappointment that it might have been better.

I then play out a different scenario for them. Had they said £20 and I said no way, £200, and they say, *"No, £20"* . . ., £150, "No £20", £100, "No £20" etc. and eventually we end up at £20, they *feel* fantastic. They think they are a negotiating god!

In both situations they paid the exact same price, ended up at the exact same place, but how they feel about it differs massively. One they regret, with the other they are delighted. One they think £20 was disappointing, the other not.

At some time in your life you will probably have had the experience where you have bought something at a great price (received a discount or whatever) and are really happy with your deal. You are then telling friends about it and the great deal you struck, when one of them says, "Why didn't you tell me? I have a relative who works there and could have got you one of those for half price!"

Your great deal now feels like a rubbish deal! However, all that has changed is how you feel about it, not how much you paid.

In the iPad example, what makes it feel so bad in the first instance is that it seemed way too easy. What felt much better in the second instance is the amount of work that had to be put in to get the deal. It wasn't easy to get there. If it's too easy it doesn't feel good and if it doesn't feel good it isn't win/win.

We should genuinely strive for win/win. No party should feel beaten. At the same time, we need to realise that win/win is a feeling not a point. The skill is to help someone feel good about where they end up and know they made the right decision. Read on and see how.

CHAPTER SUMMARY

1. Always strive for a win/win.

2. Win/win is *anywhere* both parties are happy.

3. Win/win moves around based on circumstances.

4. Win/win is a *feeling,* not a point

CHAPTER FOUR

GOLDEN RULE NO· 4

"It has to look like it hurts"

"Getting you to reduce your fees should be like pulling teeth, not taking candy from a baby"

AUTHOR

There is a very simple piece of human psychology we all understand and appreciate – we tend to be more satisfied by, and prouder of, things which were difficult to accomplish; challenges overcome, goals attained, tough times worked through, races run, homes bought, mountains climbed, weight lost, clients won, and so on. When things are too easy we simply do not value them as much.

This simple psychological trait has a profound effect on negotiation.

Using the iPad example again, let's consider why the feeling about the outcome changes after the protracted negotiation and not after the immediate deal. Two reasons:

1. They had to *work* for it.
2. It looked like it was hurting me.

It is a sad indictment on the human condition (and not one which I am advocating) that a primary reason why the feeling was different in the second instance is that it seemed I was hurting and that they were in some way beating me.

The plain fact of the matter is that if it comes across as being too easy then people are not satisfied. If you immediately change your terms after little pressure, it doesn't feel good enough to the other person, so they continue to ask for more.

When I started my career in Procter & Gamble, I was doing "deals" with major national retailers worth £millions – but it wasn't my money. Furthermore, I was selling major market leading brands with £millions of backing and advertising support. So to be fair I was in a strong position to start with.

It wasn't until I set up my own business, Whitewater International Training & Consultancy (now Maclemons International), that I really began to understand what selling and negotiating were. If I wanted to build my business, or at the other end of the scale, to eat, I had to be better at it. If you own your recruiting business this is no doubt a concept with which you are familiar.

Most sales forces I train are playing with someone else's money to a greater or lesser degree.

The huge difference for recruiters is that most often they are rewarded primarily on some form of commission, so when they do take their fees down they are actually handing over their own money and income.

As such they are agreeing with the other party that their service is not worth what is being asked, opening up their own wallet and handing the other party real cash they could have kept for themselves.

For you as a recruiter it should hurt you to be so willing to give your own money away. As stated in the chapter heading, getting you to reduce your fees should be like pulling teeth, not taking candy from a baby!

I am not for one minute suggesting some form of acting routine for the client whereby you raise the back of your hand to your forehead and cry, "Woe is me, I have a mortgage to pay, you are killing me." But, you should be willing to defend your position, pricing and service to the nth degree and feel seriously bad about handing over your own money. The more you do this, the more the other party has to work, the more it appears that it hurts you, the better the other party feels. Fact.

There are four key ways to show more pain, one of which is peculiar to the recruitment industry:

1. Talk cash not percentages.
2. Move in smaller increments.

3. Move in decreasing sized increments.
4. Use a very specific, odd number.

Let me explain.

1. Talk cash not percentages

The language of the recruitment industry is percentages – 25%, 15% whatever. The problems as I see it with using percentages are threefold:

i. Most people don't understand them (and a huge number of recruiters I have met don't understand them either).
ii. The numbers will always look small.
iii. You are easily compared to your competitors.

The evidence I have for most people not understanding percentages is simple. You may not believe what I am about to say but I can assure you it's true. I also apologise if you think the next piece is ridiculously basic and you are good with numbers.

I ask every group, if you move from terms of business of 25% to a 20% fee, how much have you moved? To my astonishment many people reply "5%".

No, it's a 20% move not a 5% move. Going from 25% to 20% is cutting your fees by 20%. (If you are a bit confused by this you really need to ask someone to explain it to you!). For the sake of argument, if you were going to make £250 from that placement personally (not as the whole fee), you have just handed over £50 of your own money. Now imagine the number of roles you do like that and how much cash is rolling out of your life.

In addition, often the client doesn't really understand the above principle either! How many clients or customers do *they* have to whom they would automatically give 20% off their own pricing? Very few. But it looks like you gave them 5% and that is what they think you gave them.

A further problem in dealing with percentages as your language is they will always look small as numbers (the largest really possible being 100). For ease of understanding, let's say the whole 25% fee is worth £5,000 and you move to 20%. Which is more enticing? You saying you will only charge 20% or you saying you could possibly, at a push, take £1,000 off the invoice? It sounds so much bigger and more enticing and looks like a much bigger win for the client.

In addition, because everyone in recruitment talks percentages, if competitors have offered 20% fee and you have offered to take £1,000 off, the chances are your offer looks better against theirs and is also harder to compare instantaneously.

Stop talking percentages and start talking cash when the numbers look in your favour.

One last thing about talking money and percentages. As a seller you should always talk money as explained above but when you are buying always ask for percentage discounts! If you ask for just 10% off it doesn't sound like you are asking for much. If the price for a car is £30,000 and you ask for just 10% off, that is £3,000!! It sounds like a small ask but is worth a lot. It is the same principle but in reverse!

2. Move in smaller increments

Our natural human instinct is to look for ordered shape and form. We naturally put two items on a mantelpiece with one at either end. Or if it's three items, we place one in the middle. If we have three lane options on a road, most people naturally sit in the middle one (which is incredibly annoying, causes traffic build up and is now illegal thank goodness – get left!).

With numbers, we like to calculate in easy chunks – 5s and 10s being the most obvious ones. It is far easier to count in 5s and 10s, 50s and 100s.

This all sounds great but is potentially a lethal trap for recruiters. Let's say terms of business are 25%. I have witnessed many people moving to 20% as their first move! Why? Because it's easy to do and understand! Sadly, I have then witnessed the next move under pressure being straight to 15% for the same reasons. What happened to all the numbers in between?

Why were reductions in fees in such huge jumps, missing out all the other potential options? Where did 24%. 23%, 22% etc all disappear to? Move in smaller increments! Use those other numbers in between. Move in 1s and 2s, not 5s! Even use half percentage points.

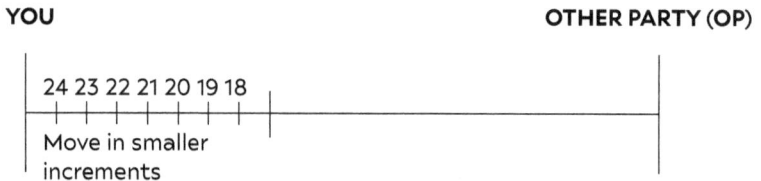

YOU   **OTHER PARTY (OP)**

24 23 22 21 20 19 18

Move in smaller
increments

3. Move in decreasing sized increments

Imagine a situation where I am selling you a second-hand car and you start to haggle. I know that I will be happy to give £500 off the selling price, but you don't.

If I say I can give you £125 off, but you keep haggling, I then say I could give you a further £100 off, but you keep going and then I say, another £50 off would be all I could do – each movement is getting smaller. What do you think that signals to you? You start to believe I am genuinely running out of room to manoeuvre and are getting me to my best price, simply by the fact each move is getting smaller – thus you are happy. So far I have given £275 off. For the sheer fun of it you have one last go at haggling me down and after much ado I say I could give you £25 for fuel and that's it!

As a result of moving in decreasing sized increments, each time it feels better to you as it appears it is increasingly hurting me. You are happy. I have given £300 to you and still have £200 for myself!

In the recruitment world, therefore, if you must use percentages (although I recommend you try to avoid it) if you can move from a 25% fee to a fee of 23% (a move of 2), then to 22% (a move of 1), then to 21.5% (a move of 0.5), and finally, if needs be, another move of 0.5 to take you to 21%, they feel great, and you are considerably better off than if you had gone straight to 20% and been haggled down from there.

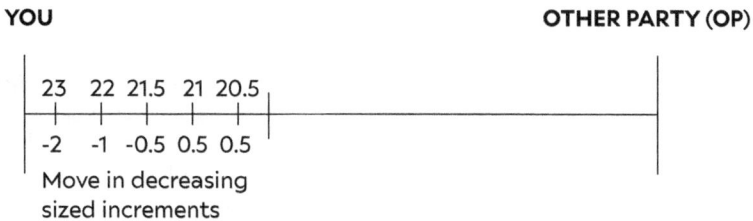

YOU   **OTHER PARTY (OP)**

23   22 21.5   21 20.5

-2   -1   -0.5 0.5 0.5

Move in decreasing
sized increments

To illustrate these various points I always tell my real-life example of going into a well-known, national electrical retailer. I had just begun to understand the principles of this book and was keen to see if they worked!

The Washing machine etc

Some time ago I had moved to a new house and needed a new washing machine / dishwasher / fridge freezer.

I went to a massive store of a national retailer with my partner who picked the items and we were joined by a salesperson. I pointed to all three items and asked how much that would be in total. The salesperson took out their calculator, added up the three prices and showed me the total.

All I said was, "That is just those 3 numbers added together. Well, I am not paying that!" I then watched him take his calculator and subtract £50 from the total. That was way too easy! £50 at first go and no pain! (* see key notes following this example.)

I asked, "How many people come in here and buy all these items at the same time on the same day?"

"Not many," he replied! Oh dear! He had just handed me another reason to push for more. He took another £50 off (still not enough pain!).

"What's the best deal you can do?" I asked.

"That's all I'm authorised to give."

BINGO! – he had just sent the signal that someone else has authority to give more! (**See key notes after the example.)

The manager came over and got involved. We discussed that we had taken the price down by £100 and he said, *"£100 off is a good deal."*

I replied, "This guy said you could do a better one . . ." (Sorry, I do now feel guilty about saying that and potentially placing the guy in trouble.)

"Well I couldn't do much better." He had just signalled that he could do better though.

"I'll give you another £50!" So we were now at £150 off.

Two big mistakes so far on their part. There was not enough pain in the process, and secondly they kept moving in big numbers – £50s! He could have said £25s even.

"That's great, all on 0% interest," I stated.

"No, only the fridge/freezer is on interest free."

"Ah, okay. We'll leave it."

"Okay, 0% over 18 months on everything."

"And free insurance!"

"No, there is no way I can do that."

"What is the best you can do on insurance?"

"Half price."

"Great, thank you!"

A key point here is that the manager did not offer me half price insurance but he said he could do it and I jumped in and accepted it as an offer! (See Golden Rule no 10 re "thank and bank".)

At this point even my partner was massively uncomfortable and tugging gently at my sleeve to stop, but I had to keep going, just for the fun of it, because it had only now looked like it was hurting. So, I asked one last question:

"What else could you throw in to make me do the deal right now?"

I am not exaggerating: the manager of this massive outlet stood in the middle of his own store and looked all around before saying, *"Ten blank video tapes." (it was a while ago!!)*

I took the deal. £150 off, 18 months interest free, half price insurance and 10 blank video tapes.

In reality I have no idea if this was a good deal or not – but I was happy, so in my world it was a good deal. That is the point. I *felt* happy.

For all I know the manager could have gone to the extent of giving me the cheapest item free but I will never know, and to be honest, it doesn't matter. I was happy.

Remember: Win/win is a *feeling* about where you end up, not the place itself.

KEY NOTES

* Top tip when buying things – always watch their calculator! The guy simply took the original total and did "minus £50". You can always tell a lot by watching what the seller does with their calculations. "Minus £50" definitely meant he had more to go. He did not even use a percentage reduction calculation. Always watch the calculator!

** It is important that if you have a boss, or are the boss, the right signals are sent.

As the boss you must support your people. If you always trump the offer of the person who works for you, two things happen:

1. You undermine your team member or employee in front of the client.
2. You train the client to talk to you instead of your team member as they know you can give better deals.

For example – If you are in a meeting with the client, ask your team member what *they* think is possible, so they are seen as the decision maker. This solidifies their credibility in the eyes of the client.

As the team member, stay away from saying you have to ask your boss. I know it is tempting. It can seem the best way to maintain a relationship is to blame someone else for not being able to do certain things – it is called "agent negotiation". However, if you say you have to ask your boss, the client might as well ask them for you! Forever after you have lost credibility and are cut out of the loop.

Instead, say you have to go away and look at the numbers, consider what is possible, and see what you can work on.

Recruitment Example

A perfect adoption of this Golden Rule was by a recruitment client following the training where a particular office decided to make a spreadsheet and have it in front of every recruiter. It had the salary bands at which particular fees kicked in and then each percentage point reduction in fees, what that meant in terms of the entire fee, and more importantly, what it meant in income to the recruiter themselves. They could see in black and white if they moved, exactly how much it was costing them. They started to feel a *whole lot more pain* in moving and it transformed their negotiating stance. Try it!

4. Use a very specific, ODD, number

This is such an easy tactic to employ and works on a very simple piece of human psychology.

Remember above we talked about how people like to count in easy numbers? 5s, 10s etc? Well there is another way you can use this to your advantage. It is best illustrated by a very simple example.

Let's say we were negotiating together and I was the seller. I have put forward a price of £10,000. You are haggling hard however. If I eventually, after moving in small and decreasing sized chunks, all of a sudden suggested £8,967.09 as my last offer, what does it suggest to you?

Because the number is so specific it suggests proper thought has gone into it and you have pushed me to the limit. And if that is what you think, you are happy! And if you are happy, you won.

It only works with ODD numbers though, the reason being if it was an even number it would have been easy to work out. It is the odd-ness and specificity of it that makes this tactic work!

CHAPTER SUMMARY

1. You must show pain.

2. Getting you to take your fees down should be like pulling teeth not taking candy from a baby.

3. Talk cash not percentages.

4. Move in smaller increments

5. Move in decreasing sized increments.

6. Use a very specific odd number

Always be the owner of your own negotiations, rather than leaving it to your boss

CHAPTER FIVE

GOLDEN RULE NO· 5

"You have to know when to walk out,
before you walk in!"

"A fundamental of successful negotiation is that you
have to know when to walk out, before you walk in!"

———

AUTHOR

Where most individuals are caught out and end up on the wrong end of a bad deal is they don't know when to walk away. They don't already know the figures, fees or rates at which they are not going to work. It is imperative to know before any negotiation just how far you are willing to go to secure the business.

EXAMPLE

The crazy deal I never should have done.

When I first started my own business in 1999, like any normal person I wanted to have a great client list and work with companies who would help build the reputation of the services we could offer.

It was at this point I was approached to do a decent sized project for one of the world's top two strategic consultancies. Wow, what an opportunity to have their name on the client list! Off I went to meet with the client and by the time I came out I had given a 75% reduction on the rates I had started from. 75% off? Are you kidding me? That is like you as a recruiter going in at a 25% starting point fee and agreeing to do the work for 6.25%! Totally insane. Utterly bonkers.

The problem was I didn't know when to walk out *before* I walked in. Most people come to the same conclusion, after it's too late. They realise when they *should have* walked out, on the way out!

I was tortured by my lack of spine. Of course I wanted them as a client, but I had basically rolled over and had my tummy tickled, devaluing what I could do to an extraordinary degree. Each day I worked on that project for those ridiculous fees I beat myself up, until one night, standing in my kitchen, whilst having a conversation with myself in my head, I blurted out, "I am never doing that again, ever!"

(The problem with conversations in your head, of course, is that when you then say something out loud, anyone around you is pretty confused!!) "Never doing what exactly?" I was asked.

"I am never going to take my fees down like that ever again. Never. I never want to feel this stupid and cheap again."

So, that night, in my kitchen, I set a fee. A fee I would resolutely never go below. A fee I could not be negotiated past because I had decided I couldn't. From then on I would know when to walk away. I can truthfully say that to this day, I have never gone past that point.

Having a walk-away point gives you confidence. If you already know you will not, and cannot, be forced to a point you don't want to go, there is an immediate sense of safety and self-belief which transforms your capabilities in any negotiation situation.

In the recruitment world time and again I have seen situations where people have made insane agreements at crazy rates. They then expend a massive amount of energy internally in their own company talking about how they are playing the long strategic game and the idea is to get in to the client, spread their influence, and then negotiate rates up, blah blah blah. That is nuts, plain and simple.

We all know this does not work. You must know what it is like to take over a client from someone else who has gone in at suicidal rates and you have had to try to negotiate them up. How easy is that exactly? Impossible.

Stop kidding yourself that this works because it doesn't. The aim should be to rely heavily on your selling skills and when you then have to negotiate, negotiate hard and well to keep rates up the first time around. Over time, if the client is doing their negotiation job properly, they will continuously put pressure on to drive rates down, and at least you have some leeway within which to operate.

| YOU | Walk-away point. Wherever you decide it is. You are not going past this point. | OTHER PARTY (OP) |

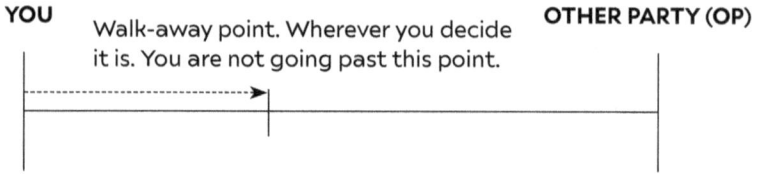

Another key factor of your walk-away point being in place is that you know you can stay in some level of control. No matter how bombastic the client, or how unreasonable they are, you know that you will not have to leave with that feeling of "oh dear, I don't think I should have done that"! If you are being honest with yourself, you know you have done this before, as have I.

So, what was the reason I caved in so easily in my example? I wanted the client and I had a conviction you always have to take any work at any price. Now I know I said in chapter 1 that every job counts, and it does, but with some perspective. If you are the business owner of a recruitment company, or a senior level executive in a larger business, you need to make up your mind about what your strategy is. If it is simply to grab any work you can at any rates you can, fair enough. Know that you will pretty much always have a low margin business and go for volume.

If, however, your goal is to have great people doing a great job for a worthy reward, you have to permit those people to walk away from some business. They have to be properly trained to be able to, and have the blessing to, negotiate hard. If the client expectations are plain unreasonable, you have to support their stance of not committing margin suicide.

I have been quite lucky in the many great recruiters I have met. They tell me over and over again about how some clients wanted an insanely low rate, said they could get the same candidates elsewhere etc. and they were way too expensive. The recruiters in question did the professional and smart thing. They said that unfortunately at those rates they would not be able to help but they would certainly want to help should the client not find what they were looking for. What happens the vast majority of the time? The client comes back.

Yet another use of the walk-away point is to be able to put into practice principles from Golden Rule No 5. If you know the point past which you refuse to go, the closer you get to it, the more pain you naturally show. You can also move in decreasing or smaller increments to move towards it instead of giant leaps.

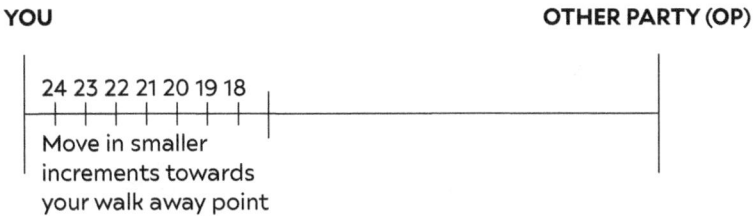

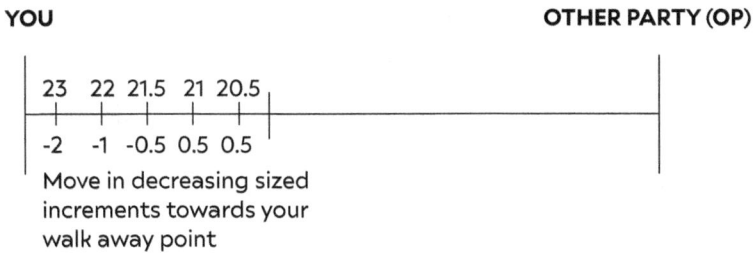

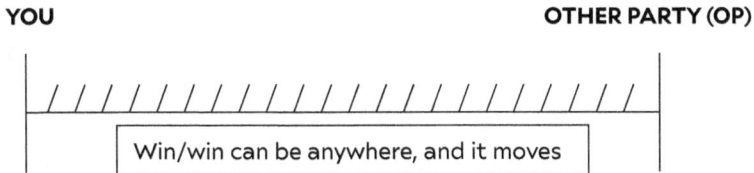

YOU   **OTHER PARTY (OP)**

24 23 22 21 20 19 18

Move in smaller
increments towards
your walk away point

YOU   **OTHER PARTY (OP)**

23   22 21.5 21 20.5

-2   -1 -0.5 0.5 0.5

Move in decreasing sized
increments towards your
walk away point

YOU   **OTHER PARTY (OP)**

Win/win can be anywhere, and it moves

EXAMPLE

Recruitment

Remember the office that did the spreadsheet from the last chapter? The other thing they did was agree together that no matter who was offered work in that office, there was an agreed walk-away point. No difference from one consultant to another and a fixed point below which no one would go. What do you think happened? Well, truthfully, their number of jobs went down – but their margin went way up. They were doing fewer roles, for more money and offsetting the drop in volume. Powerful stuff.

CHAPTER SUMMARY

1. You have to know when to walk out, before you walk in.

2. A predetermined walk-away point gives you confidence.

3. A walk-away point by nature means the closer you get to it, the more pain you show.

4. Going in low, and trying to then negotiate up never works.

5. Move in smaller increments towards your walk-away point.

6. Move in decreasing sized increments towards your walk away point.

7. Make your walk away point a very specific odd number.

CHAPTER SIX

GOLDEN RULE NO· 6

"When stuck, chunk up"

*"We could not have found peace, unless the
desire for it was already there"*
_____
COLUM MCCANN

When negotiation proceedings seem to have ground to a halt, with neither party willing to move, the key thing to focus the minds of everyone concerned upon is the common ground. What is it you are both trying to achieve?

Often, particularly in tense negotiations, parties can begin to dig into their own positions, creating what is akin to World War 1 trench warfare. In recruitment these positions are often denoted by numbers – percentages: fees you want to charge and fees the OP is apparently only prepared to pay.

Let's take an example

YOU		OTHER PARTY (OP)
25%		12%

You say your fees are 25% and they say no way – it has to be 12%. It appears pretty impossible they will pay 25% and there is no way at all you are going to halve your fee to 12%. Now what?

Northern Ireland

Being from Northern Ireland I often use the peace process there (at a macro level) to best illustrate the Golden Rule "When stuck, chunk up". Whilst I have consciously mentioned at the very beginning of the book not to see negotiation as having "sides", I will use the word in this example, as I believe it helps illustrate the point.

I think it would be fair to say that historically there have been 'differing points of view and subsequent differences of opinion' in the province! Long-standing ones at that. So with such polarized "sides", with entrenched belief systems, and absolutely no hope whatsoever of either side ever accepting the other's position or acquiescing to their stance, what can you do? How on earth do you ever create a situation whereby a peace process can even be started, let alone accomplished?

The secret? Constantly keeping those concerned focused on the common goals they have, and not the starting positions they are coming from.

What was in the interest of both sides? What did they both want? – peace. By focusing on a goal both parties want to achieve, it becomes less important as to where you are starting from and can help break deadlock.

So how do you create this focused attention? – **"Chunk up"**!

Diagram 1

YOU   CHUNK UP   OTHER PARTY (OP)

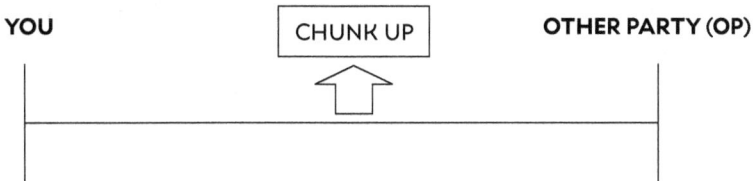

Normally I gain a few laughs and giggles at this point for even using the expression "Chunk up". It is actually a proper term coming from the world of Neuro Linguistic Programming (NLP) and originally borrowed from the world of information technology.

Chunking is a very simple principle to understand and involves either getting out of the detail to see the bigger picture (chunking up), or having to become involved in more detail or break it down in to smaller pieces (chunking down).

Chunking up is about seeing the bigger picture, taking more of a helicopter view and gaining a broader perspective; putting things in an overall context. It is needed when people find themselves too immersed in the minutiae of a situation; too conscious of, and focused upon, the small details, and becoming bogged down. Somewhat akin to "they can't see the wood for the trees". Think of it like this. If someone is lost but has a map, a good first step is trying to get to high ground to pick out landmarks. That way the map itself starts to make sense. Just staring at the detail on the map alone probably won't help.

Chunking down is in contrast. When people are faced with a huge situation or seemingly insurmountable challenge, the smart thing to do is chunk down; break it down into smaller constituent parts so that the smaller pieces are more easily dealt with. As the old adage goes "you can eat an elephant, but just not in one sitting"!

So when stuck in positions (detail) it is important to be able to chunk up, eloquently talk about the bigger picture and what both parties are trying to achieve overall in order to make it obvious how a win/win outcome is still possible and preferable.

For example, if the client has a role or roles needing to be filled, tell them you are convinced you can successfully do that in the time-scales they wish, if not faster, and have total confidence you will fulfil the brief. Then ask, "What are the costs of delaying the hires?" "How pressurized is the need to get this done?" "As a result what are the consequences of sitting arguing over small numbers versus getting the roles filled and the business moving forward?"

The Prisoner's Dilemma

One way to successfully chunk up in stuck negotiation situations is to use the "Prisoner's Dilemma". Look up those two words on the internet and you can be reading for days. Now anyone who has done any research on negotiation, and doesn't know about the prisoner's dilemma, is, to say the least, not very well informed. However, even though I knew the model as a principle, I didn't know how to use it practically, until the example below.

I will briefly explain the concept but read up on it, as well as "Game Theory", if you want to go for a really deep dive into the world of negotiation.

According to the Concise Encyclopaedia of Economics – "The prisoner's dilemma is the best known game of strategy in social science. It helps us understand what governs the balance between cooperation and competition in business, politics, and in social settings . . . The concept of the Prisoner's Dilemma was developed by RAND Corporation scientists Merrill Flood and Melvin Dresher and was formalized by Albert Tucker, a Princeton mathematician."

Here is my quick explanation of the model and then I will go on to show its practical application. As I say there is endless information on the Prisoners' Dilemma and much more in depth than I am about to impart.

See the diagram overleaf as you read the explanation.

One way of explaining the dilemma is simple – two criminals are arrested by the Police for being involved in the same crime. Are they put in the same cell? No. Why not? They could collude with each other and put a story together. They are parted, placed in two separate cells, and this is where the dilemma kicks in.

Both prisoners, prisoner A and prisoner B have choices to make. They intrinsically know it is in both their interests for both of them to say nothing at all to the authorities. This can result in the best possible outcome – possibly getting away with it!

However, each prisoner also knows something else:

> If A says nothing, and B confesses, turning state witness, A will receive a worse sentence than B because of being unhelpful and a recalcitrant holdout.

> Conversely, if B says nothing, and A confesses, A wins for being helpful and B loses.

So here is the $1,000,000 question: If they both know that saying nothing could end up with them both getting away with it, but also know confessions can protect themselves a little, what happens in the vast majority of cases? Yup – they both confess – even though if they both said nothing they might walk away free.

Why? In essence, because the outcome most beneficial to them both is based on trust and that involves both people, not just one. They are not in total control of the best possible outcome, so they go for the outcome they can control – confessing – which is sub-optimal.

Diagram 2

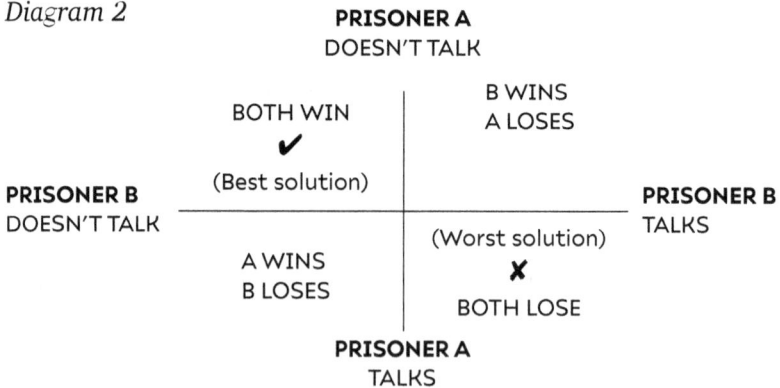

PRISONER A
DOESN'T TALK

BOTH WIN
✔
(Best solution)

B WINS
A LOSES

PRISONER B
DOESN'T TALK

PRISONER B
TALKS

A WINS
B LOSES

(Worst solution)
✗
BOTH LOSE

PRISONER A
TALKS

So what in the world does that have to do with you as a recruiter sitting in front of a client when negotiations are stalling? Allow me to explain.

EXAMPLE

The Bar in Cape Town

I was in a bar in Cape Town of all places shortly after developing the basic outline of the 12 Golden Rules when out of the blue a former colleague of mine from Procter & Gamble UK walked in. Small world! After all the pleasantries Tony and I ended up talking about what we were both up to nowadays, and I explained I was focusing a lot of attention on my newly-developed model for easily explaining negotiation. We were in animated discussion for some time until I came to Golden Rule No 6 whereupon he said, "You ought to use the prisoner's dilemma there!"

Of course I knew the model but I thought it was a bit unnecessary to go into its detail for the purposes of my trainings. Whilst it was a fundamental basis of what I was talking about, I wanted to keep the programme practical; real world tools to actually use, say and do.

However, what Tony gave me was amazing. He gave me a simple way to use it in front of customers. A simple way to use such a powerful model in a non-aggressive, totally collaborative and, most importantly, very persuasive manner to help both parties in a stalling negotiation find a win/win outcome.

So, on the back of a beer mat (I am not kidding!), he showed me how to talk through the model in a meeting, to great advantage, for the benefit of both parties. Loved it! Thanks, Tony. Here we go:

Draw the framework on a piece of paper and build it as follows

1) **Draw the axis below**

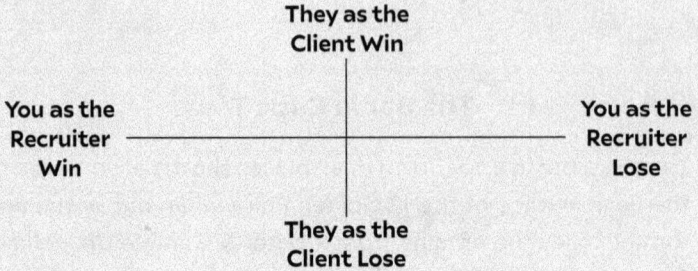

2) **Build up your explanation as follows:**

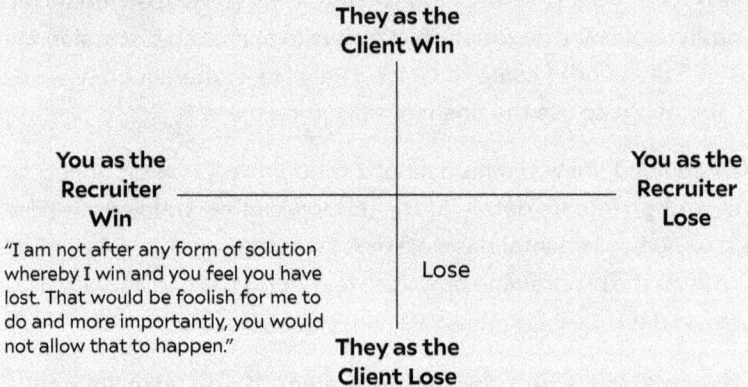

3)

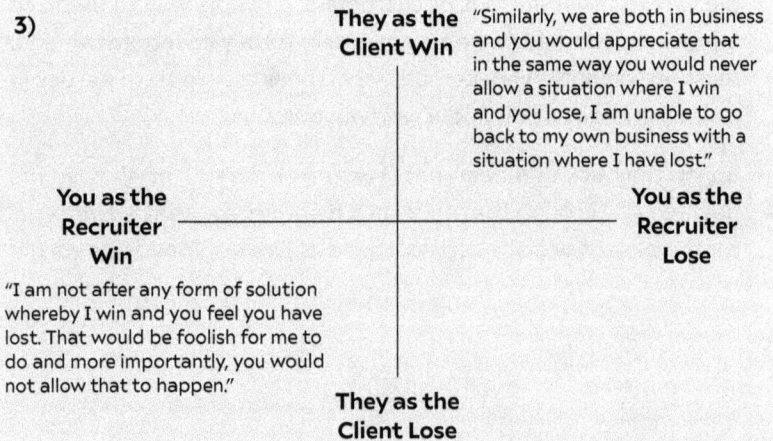

4)

They as the Client Win — "Similarly, we are both in business and you would appreciate that in the same way you would never allow a situation where I win and you lose, I am unable to go back to my own business with a situation where I have lost."

You as the Recruiter Win ——————————— **You as the Recruiter Lose**

"I am not after any form of solution whereby I win and you feel you have lost. That would be foolish for me to do and more importantly, you would not allow that to happen."

"I think it would be a real shame if we couldn't find a way whereby we are both happy, and I really think us not finding a way forward would be a genuine loss to us both."

They as the Client Lose

5)

They as the Client Win — "Similarly, we are both in business and you would appreciate that in the same way you would never allow a situation where I win and you lose, I am unable to go back to my own business with a situation where I have lost."

"So all I am trying to do here is sincerely find a win/win result – an outcome acceptable to us both. Would you be interested in finding that?"

You as the Recruiter Win ——————————— **You as the Recruiter Lose**

"I am not after any form of solution whereby I win and you feel you have lost. That would be foolish for me to do and more importantly, you would not allow that to happen."

"I think it would be a real shame if we couldn't find a way whereby we are both happy, and I really think us not finding a way forward would be a genuine loss to us both."

They as the Client Lose

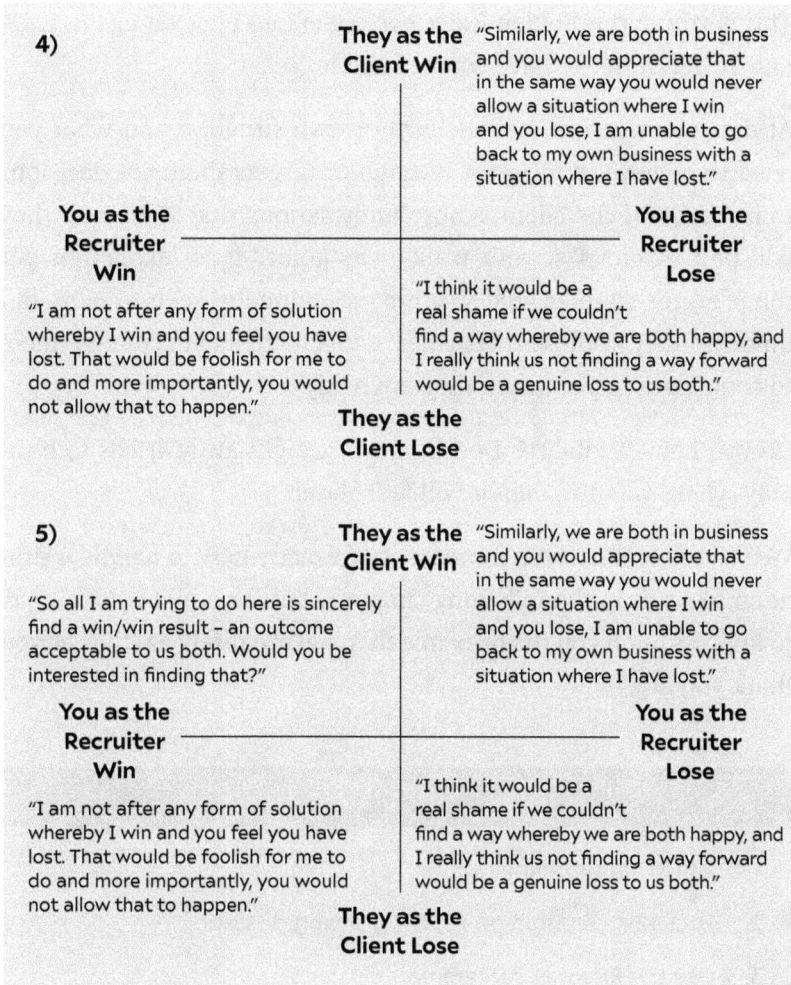

By the time you get to the end of talking through the diagram, and have asked if they would be interested in finding a win/win solution, if you hear any other word than "no", the chances are they can move and there is some room to manoeuvre!

So what else can you do in these types of stuck situations?

This is where the Golden Rules can come into play yet again. Even only using those we have covered so far.

At that moment in time versus your own situation and what you need to achieve in terms of revenue or targets there are decisions to be made. If the client is absolutely serious that 12% is all they will pay, is that past your walk-away point? If so, explain as per the previous chapter, that you are exceptionally keen to help, but unfortunately at those rates you are unable to and encourage them to come back to you when they are ready.

Do you have flexibility? Do not move straight away. It has to hurt. Stay where you are, then it will feel better.

We start to look at even more ways of exactly how to handle a situation like this in the following chapters, but for now I want simply to impress upon you the principle that you are rarely as stuck as you think you are.

CHAPTER SUMMARY

1. When stuck, chunk up!

2. Focus on common goals, not starting positions.

3. Use the Prisoner's Dilemma.

4. If the demands are past your walk-away point – walk away.

5. If you *have* to move, make the OP work for it – it will feel better to them.

CHAPTER SEVEN

GOLDEN RULE NO· 7

"You must know the variables"

"The best move you can make in negotiation is to think of an incentive the other person hasn't even thought of – and then meet it."

———

ELI BROAD

A vital point to realise is you are <u>never</u> negotiating with what things cost; you are <u>always</u> negotiating with what things are worth. There is a <u>big</u> difference.

For example. Have you ever been burgled? Of the items taken, what upset you most? The most expensive things? 99% of the time it is the things of sentimental value – the things which can't be replaced are those which most distress people.

What does it cost to print a photograph? Let's say 15 pence at most. Would you like to buy a photograph of me? Not even for 15p? Probably not.

However, if it is a great photograph of you or your loved ones, would you only pay 15p?

It is not the *cost* of the photograph that matters; it is how *valuable* it is to you.

The difference between cost and value is the absolute basis of all negotiation, yet most recruiters do not know what they have to negotiate with, or the cost or value of what they would want in return.

Without knowing these things it is unwise even to start to negotiate, as you have no clue what you are doing, and someone who does will probably be able to take advantage.

Let's look at another example, this time to illustrate cost and value and also how it is intrinsically linked to Golden Rule No 3 – win/win.

EXAMPLE

The Water in the Desert

Imagine you are lost in the desert and dying of dehydration. You have pockets full of money, but no water.

You suddenly meet someone who has a bottle of water, which for the sake of argument cost them £1. Would you only be willing to pay £1 for it? You know it only cost £1 but right now its value to you is massively bigger.

At that point you would pay anything . . .

So you pay £1,000 for it. An hour later you crest a sand dune and there is a beautiful oasis, beautiful pool of water, palm trees, the lot.

Having dived into the water, cooled down, had a drink and taken shelter under a palm tree, the same person comes along with another bottle of water and offers it to you for another £1,000. Same bottle, same cost, but now its value to you is hugely different. You don't need it as much so you might say "no way, go away".

If the water seller is smart, though, they would try to sell you an empty bottle, because whilst you have lots of water now at the oasis, you can't carry much of it if you want to move on. His water has gone down in value but his bottle has gone up!

So when negotiating there are things you have which the OP might want, and things they have you would want. In negotiation literature they are often called tradables or variables. Let us use "variables" as they are the pieces of the puzzle or deal which you and the OP can vary.

Your Variables – what do you have to negotiate with?

Taking your variables first, each one has a cost to you of doing it, and a value to the other party of receiving it, i.e. how much it actually costs you to give that variable, and how valuable it is in the eyes of the OP to be getting it.

For ease, let's give each a summary value of low / medium / or high

Low (L) / medium (M) / high (H) cost to you to give it, and

L / M / H value to the other party to receive it, like the table below.

YOUR VARIABLES

Your variables to Trade	Cost to you to give it L/M/H	Value to the other party to receive it L/M/H
PRICE	H	H

What most recruiters do is cave in to pressure on price, and way too quickly. Cost to you to do that is high, value to the other person to get it is high.

I have heard it relentlessly across the globe that all the buyer is interested in is price. Our rates are too high, we are uncompetitive – the type of thinking which accelerates the race to the bottom.

I have even witnessed situations where consultants will actively avoid talking about rates and will send the client the terms of business in the post in the hope they won't notice! This is nothing but a recipe for disaster. When the client receives the terms, they are unhappy and refuse to pay, and the worst part is the candidate has already been placed. You can't walk back in to the client, take the candidate who has a great new role in which they are happy, and tell them they have to leave because the client isn't paying! The candidate is placed and the recruiter no longer has any leverage to negotiate with. Now it simply turns into a battle of wills, another client on the internal debtors list and a protracted argument, which at worst goes legal.

However, there are so many other things recruiters have at their disposal which can be offered in a deal other than, or rather than, a reduction in fees; things which cost little to provide and do, but offer real value to the client.

***

N.B. I am aware that in some of the cases I will list below you might disagree, either with the rating of cost or value (L/M/H), a variable has been given, or even with the existence of the variable itself. The value of particular variables may also differ with different clients.

***

This, however, is not supposed to be the exhaustive and absolute list of variables for you or your industry. This is merely a guide or a means of sparking the thought process as to what the correct variables and values would be for you and your business. Make your own list if needs be. The key is to have a list of variables you know you have, and some idea as to how valuable they are to the clients you deal with every day.

KNOW YOUR VARIABLES

Your Variables to Trade	Cost to You to give it	Value to the OP to receive it
Reduction in fee	H	H
Extended guarantee period;	L	H
Changing your payment terms. Delayed invoice or split invoice	M	M
Meetings	H	H
Testing	L	H
Providing interview facilities	L	M / H
Re-interviews	L	H

Referencing	L	H
Qualification checks	L	H
Resignation management	L	M
Giving the offer	L	M
Salary advice	L	M
Post placement care	L	M
Outplacements	L	M
Sit in on interview	L	M
Washing up after interview	L	M
Promoting their business	L	H
Preparing the candidate	L	M
Feedback at each stage	L	H
Competency based interview help	L	H
Benchmarking	L	H
Mailings	L	M / H
Targeted searches	L	M / H
Competitor information	L	M / H
Exclusive candidates	L	M / H
Niche knowledge	L	M / H
Guarantee to fill the job in a particular timescale, and if not the fee drops	L / M	H
National searches	L	M / H
International searches	L	M / H
Feedback on their organisation	L	M / H
Free web job on your sites if you have one	L	M
Discounted adverts	L	H
Handling advert responses	L	M / H
Extended working interview	L	M
Potentially differentiate your fees on seniority. For you as a senior person handling the role, the fee is higher, or you can drop the fee by giving the role to a more junior person	L	M / H

Do you see a pattern here? Do you see how many things other than a reduction in price could be brought in to a negotiation? More importantly, look at how so many of them cost you little to give but could be so valuable to the OP!

Like many others you may now be thinking, "but we do all this already. A lot of these are things we do as a matter of course". The issue is, however, they are not talked about with the client. Going back to Golden Rule No 1, people buy from someone where they can see the value in it. These extras, if you like, the variables you already have included in your fee, must be talked about openly to show where the value in your service lies. The others you can then put into play as part of a negotiation, and we will explore exactly how in Golden Rule No 8.

Even the way you talk about a variable can transform its value in the eyes of the OP.

In my Negotiation Skills programme I never give out a binder or folder full of PowerPoint slides for delegates to take away. This is for two main reasons:

1. There is no deck of PowerPoint slides I show. It is all through examples, flipcharts and insight sessions.
2. Binders are a complete waste of time, energy, paper and money. Most are never opened or used again after the course and one delegate even confessed that one of their training binders was now holding up the corner of their wardrobe!

Instead, what every delegate receives is an A5 laminated card with all the key information and Golden Rules upon it – easily carried and referred to. I have been told over and over again how much more useful this is and have met delegates years later who still have theirs with them and use it often.

Let me confess, however, to a situation whereby I got it completely wrong when talking about this potentially valuable item to a possible new client

---

EXAMPLE

The Laminate

I was pitching for business to a new client. Usually what I would say in my pitch is what I talked about above – we don't give binders or folders to delegates because they are never opened or used again, and instead we give delegates this great *aide memoire* in the form of an A5 laminate with all the key information. This way it stays with the individual, is easily referred to, and lasts.

However, this time around I missed out the part as to why binders do not work and why they are a waste. I simply took out the laminate and said that all delegates receive one of these.

The other person responded – *"Is that all?"* They then reached down and produced what can only be described as the "mother ship of all binders"! Huge, tabulated, colour-coded, the lot.

"One of your competitors gives each individual one of these!"

Instead of me then talking about the difference between the two, and relying on the ability to explain the difference in *value* between them, I wrongly and somewhat curtly replied, "What is it you want? A big binder or a real change in behaviour?"

Needless to say, I didn't win that work!

The problem lay with me, though. If I had asked the person right at the start if they had ever received binders on other courses and asked what had become of them, the probability is they would have responded like everyone else, to say they have never been looked at again. That way, my laminate would have had value, but I didn't talk about it and illustrate it as being something of value – so it didn't have any in the eyes of the OP.

The Clock

Another example from someone else who truly opened my eyes to the difference in playing variables with value is from when I trained the entire sales force of a major drinks company and global brand in Ireland to negotiate. At the time, this business and its sales force were experiencing seismic shifts in the market and were struggling to deal with such a changing environment.

I went with one of the sales force (for the sake of argument – Jack) to a particularly renowned and belligerent customer (Fred) who was famous for playing hardball and being considerably unreasonable. When I say unreasonable – I mean off the scale unreasonable.

The drinks company was (and still is) famous for making great branded items to be used by customers and consumers alike.

The customer (Fred) had been in a rival pub and seen a beautiful branded clock on the wall. Upon Jack and me entering, without so much as a polite hello, he barked, "Get me a clock – I want one of those clocks like 'so and so' has!"

Jack replied that they were very rare and he would have diffi-culty sourcing one, to which the customer responded in typically belligerent fashion, with what can only be described as "highly colourful language" and a further order to get him one.

When we left, I asked Jack what he thought his chances were of sourcing one of the clocks. He replied, "I already have one!" However, he explained it was the only new one he was going to receive for use on his territory and he needed to think carefully about how to gain maximum use from it across the sales area for which he was responsible.

So why did he not simply tell the customer he would get one for him?

... *"If I give it to him now, just like that, he won't value the fact I only have one and he will simply demand other things over and over again."*

The sales person, already in possession of the clock, visited the client a further four times, receiving numerous chastisements and verbal barrages from the customer in their usual extraordinary style, before he eventually stated that he thought he could get the clock.

However, he then said to the client he would need a larger order in return (see Golden Rule No. 8) and also bravely asked for a change in attitude from Fred! The larger order, as well as other concessions were agreed, the attitude was dropped, and the customer received his clock.

The sales person intrinsically understood the difference between the cost of the clock and how to enhance the value of the clock in the other person's eyes. He only had one clock so he was going to make sure he made the most from having it. Had he just handed it over, it would have been seen as of little value to the other party.

He talked about the variable in a way that gave it value.

Same clock, same cost, different value.

It was so long ago I cannot remember Jack's real name, but I can assure you I have never forgotten his wisdom.

So why all these examples? It is to show two things:

1. Any recruiter has much more to negotiate with than price, but they simply do not talk about it.
2. The way you talk about what you have, and can do, changes the value of what you have in the other person's eyes. See what order to put offers in, in Golden Rule No. 8.

Other Party's Variables – what do they have you would want in return?

So, we have looked at the various things we have to negotiate with, now let's see what the other party has we would want in return.

The most obvious is the work – we want the work! However, there are so many other things supremely useful to gain which we could also receive from the customer, as well as the work.

Yet again, let's do our table.

The client has variables which now have a cost to them to give you, and a value to you to receive. We will use our L / M / H gauge for both again. So, apart from the work, what else could the client give you?

CLIENT VARIABLES TO TRADE

Their Variables to trade	Cost to them to give you	Value to You to receive
The fee	H	H
Agreeing to no guarantee period	M	H
Them changing their payment terms	M / H	H
Money up front. Non-returnable percentage of the fee	M / H	H
Immediate payment upon completion	L	H
Exclusivity on the role	L	H
Testimonials	L	H
Referrals	L	H
Introduction to others in their business	L	H
Use of their logo	L	H
Link to their website	L	H
Their services in return	L	H
If permanent job, access to temporary jobs	L	H

On site presence	L	H
Them placing advertising instead of you	L	H
Them handling advertising responses instead of you	L	H
Master vendor agreement	M	H
Commitment to time agenda	L	H
Day of interview times	L	H
Interviews at their offices	L	H
Attendance at their events	L	H
Link with their society	L	H
Talk to their teams	L	H
Agreement to be put on their PSL if not already	L	H
Agreement to more work	M	H

Do you see the pattern again? Look at how many things you could gain back from a client which cost them little or nothing to give. You will only receive these things, however, if you ask for them. You have to learn to know what you want. You have to know what you want in return, to even be able to ask for it.

We will explore how to ask in the next chapter – Golden Rule No 8.

One tip I can give from my own experience is to become really familiar with about six variables you have to negotiate with, and six you would want in return, as it makes everything a little easier. Learn them and practise offering them in a particular order, as well as how to ask for what you want.

CHAPTER SUMMARY

1. You are always negotiating with what things are worth, not what they cost.

2. There are many things you have to negotiate with, other than price.

3. There are many things you could gain in return as well as the work.

4. Learn the variables, both yours and theirs.

CHAPTER EIGHT

GOLDEN RULE NO· 8

"Always trade, never give"

or

"If the fee changes, the deal changes"

▲

"Negotiation is a give-and-take process,
but being in control of the process is the only
way to be successful at it."

_____

CELSO CUKIERKAM

To repeat once again, taking your fee down until the other party says yes is not negotiating – it is discounting! The difference between the two is basic but fundamental. Discounting means fee reduction with the only outcome being given the work. Negotiation is where for any move you make, you are getting something in return. If the fee changes, the deal changes!

The point of showing and knowing the variables in the last chapter is to be able to put into practice the key principle of "Always trade, never give".

When it comes to using your own variables, the main goal is to protect your fee. This safeguards your income both in this present deal and the ones you will do with the same client in the future, as you will not have set an expectation of lower fees for future placements. This is done by offering other low cost, high value variables instead of a reduction in price. The way to do this is to say:

Example 1

"I can't do anything with the fee, but what I maybe could do is . . ." offering other variables, always low cost high value ones first. For example: "I can't do anything with the fee but if it were of interest to you, I could maybe take away all your risk by offering you an extended guarantee period on the placement?"

Example 2

When it comes to gaining some variables from the OP the phrase to use is *"I could maybe do something with the fee, and what I would need from you is . . ."* (getting something back in return).

For example: "I could maybe do something with the fee to the extent you would want, but what I would need from you is a commitment to a timeframe with guaranteed interview slots and exclusivity on the role."

It should be unacceptable to come back to the office and announce you took your fee down and you only won the work! It needs to be you won the work plus other variables from the client . . . as per the list of client variables.

We will examine in more detail how to "test offer variables" in Golden Rule No 10 which keeps you away from simply offering variables which are accepted and then you are pressed for more.

The client who didn't have the budget

EXAMPLE

I once had a client who wanted a huge amount of work from my business – after running some very successful pilot programmes. They wanted their sales force trained to sell better and negotiate better. They wanted all their managers trained to better manage and motivate their teams, and they also wanted to revamp their recruitment process. All of which are specialisms of ours.

I had fully specced up all the work and submitted a detailed proposal for all of the programmes over a set period of time to fit in with their fiscal year. This was a large amount of work at substantial fees. Everything was agreed.

However, out of the blue, I was contacted by the Finance Director of the business saying he wanted to meet. Now, in my line of work I generally only tend to deal with three people at top level. The Chief Executive (Managing Director), the Sales Director, or the HR Director, as they are generally the sponsors of the type of work we do and the ones who will be signing off the investment.

I had not met the Finance Director up to this point so it was fairly obvious to me what this discussion would be about . . . money!

Ironically, both of our diaries were so full it seemed getting us together was going to be an impossibility, but eventually we both realised we used Waterloo railway station as our London travel hub and agreed to meet in a bar at Waterloo, after office hours, to have our discussion. The conversation went like this:

"David, we are really excited about doing this work. We really need it and you are the business to help us. However, we just cannot afford the prices you are asking. It is a non-starter."

I asked him what his concerns were exactly, objection handled as best I could, but it was a stonewall. Selling had to stop and negotiation had to start. The client did not want to pay.

Eventually, I asked, "What total fees would you be happy to pay?" (See Golden Rule No 9)

He replied with a figure £25,000 below our proposed fees. Quite a drop, but still the value of the entire project to us as a business was considerable.

(NB: Always trade, never give; or if the fee changes the deal changes.)

So, I went for a trade. I replied, "If you write me a cheque this month for the entire value of the whole project up front, I will reduce the fees by £25,000."

The key for the Financial Director was the total cost of the project, not when it was paid. He said, *"Deal."*

We had a drink, went on our way, and the entire six-figure sum was in our account ten days later. What the client gained was a large reduction in fees, and what we gained was a huge cashflow advantage as a smaller business.

Always trade, never give. If the fee changes, the deal changes.

All or nothing!

Another large client for Whitewater was very happy with the differences they were seeing in their organisation as a result of training and development programmes run by us. Let's call them Company A. So happy, in fact, that at an industry function they attended where their competitors were present, one of their senior executives was "slightly inebriated" and waxing lyrical about all the work we were doing for them, within earshot of their biggest competitor.

Two days later we received a telephone call from the competitor asking for a meeting. Let's call them Company B. I took along our usual presentation but wasn't even given the opportunity to show it. The executive I met from Company B simply and immediately stated that whatever we were doing with Company A, they wanted it!

I then went about describing, in a very non-specific way, the sorts of things we were doing with Company A. The vagueness was necessary to be fair to our existing client.

Company B liked the sound of it all and went about telling me how many people they had, and the sorts of timescales they had in mind. I totted up a rough total cost for the work and worked out that potentially it was going to be one of our biggest accounts.

I returned to the office overjoyed that we had potentially managed to gain such a huge assignment for the company. The elation was short-lived, however!

In our business we are very conscious of not working with competitors of our existing clients unless it has been discussed with that client. This is an ethic we take very seriously.

As such, I told Company B I would have to go to Company A, and gain their blessing. Something about which B was not amused.

Two days later I was with Company A, our existing client, telling them about what had happened and – to put it mildly – they were "quite upset"!

"If you work with them you are out of here! We can't have you giving what we regard as one of our competitive advantages to our key competitor. No way. No way at all. We will withdraw from working with you."

So, now I had one of our biggest and long-standing clients, who was very important to our business, saying they would walk away. I had another large contract right within my grasp but it seemed now it was all or nothing.

I returned to the office fairly disconsolate. A large contract within my grasp and I could not touch it. Now I was upset! To be honest, I was too close to the whole negotiation and I lost proper perspective.

(***Sometimes you will be too close to the deal. Too close to the client. Too involved. It will be a "can't see the wood for the trees" situation. That is when you need to ask a colleague for advice. Someone who is more emotionally detached. They will enable you to step back, chunk up and gain a better perspective.)

Whilst having a minor rant about the whole situation, a colleague in the business stepped in and said, *"Hang on here though, David, it is not all or nothing – there are variables."*

We sat down and worked through the situation, listing variables and coming up with a positive way forward – a way forward that ended up being far, far away from all or nothing. We took stock and leaned on the principles of this book.

1. Focus on interests, not positions or, when stuck, chunk up.
2. What are the variables?

3. Always trade, never give. Or if the fee changes, the deal changes.
4. Know your walk away point.

All of this led to a win/win outcome for all concerned.

Whilst we would never work for a direct competitor without discussing it, we did not have an exclusivity agreement with Company A forbidding this.

Whilst we had been with our client for a long time, we were looking at guaranteed revenue from Company B going forward.

We would have to walk away from a guaranteed new client ongoing, to meet client demands and expectations, worth a lot to our business.

What happened and how the variables were able to make everyone happy

In an open, honest, and transparent conversation, I went back to our client and explained all of the above. In particular, I showed the total value of the new contract and how it would be so detrimental to our business to have to turn it down, even though we had worked together for so long. I highlighted that we as a business might have to walk away.

I explained to Company A that I had done the right and ethical thing to bring this situation to their attention. I also highlighted that we did not have, nor ever had, any formal agreement not to work with competitors.

What we received

The client acknowledged that exclusivity was not a given and we agreed an additional monthly retainer payment in order to put such an exclusivity clause in place.

The client agreed to sign a contract to the value of the Company B proposal guaranteeing us the same revenue over the next 12 months, thereby protecting our income.

But here is where the knowledge of variables and all the principles of negotiation really came into play.

I am generally appalled by the standard of training, learning and development in the marketplace. Poor material, worse delivery, and an outcome that generally hurts all good learning profession-als. Instead of people seeing training courses as a real opportunity to improve and be successful, they view them as days that have to be endured and of little or no value. This is such a sad situation.

Instead of great trainers imparting easily understood, easily digested and valuably used learning, most "trainers" out there do little more than bore their audience, give them a binder to take away and have attendees leaving dismayed, disappointed and discouraged, with no useable knowledge or skills.

However, I have been on, competed against, and bought, brilliant training in my time. I knew people in the market I trusted. I knew they had great content and delivery and even though they were my competitors, I respected them.

So the last twist in the "all or nothing" tale was this. Now that I knew I had a retainer and was guaranteed the work for Company A ongoing, I approached a competitor of mine I knew was great and offered to give them the Company B contract for a finder's fee. I approached Company B, explained why I could not do the work and recommended another supplier I believed would honour their expectations. Company B was happy, and I was paid a per-centage of the fee by my competitor who did all the work.

Instead of all or nothing, thanks to the fundamentals of the Golden Rules, we actually *made* money and kept all parties happy through a total win/win for all concerned.

CHAPTER SUMMARY

1. Always Trade, Never Give. If the fee changes the deal must change.

2. You do not simply give concessions without asking for something in return.

3. There are many ways to trade in situations that seem impassable.

4. You can only successfully trade if you know the variables.

5. "I can't do anything with the fee, but what I possibly could do is . . ." (offer low cost, high value variables).

6. "I could do something with the fee, and what I would need from you is . . ." (ask for variables back).

CHAPTER NINE

GOLDEN RULE NO· 9

"What is the gap?"

*"If you don't ask, you don't get and if you
don't know what they want, don't move!"*

———

AUTHOR

Having trawled through masses of negotiation material I came across many outlines and structures for how to do it. One of these structures was sixteen steps long! Sixteen steps? I simply do not have the intellectual horsepower to remember sixteen steps, or even more importantly, to be able to work out during a negotiation discussion, which step of sixteen I am currently at! Detailed yes, but in my view, not very practical.

Most negotiation skills structures have "Preparation" as a step. I do not, and for a very simple reason. If you have not prepared, and do not already know the things listed below, then you should be going nowhere near a negotiation situation. Knowledge of the list below should be a prerequisite, and not a step in the actual negotiation process.

So what can you prepare? What can you have already done?

- Sorted out your belief systems and comfort levels
- Know your walk-away point
- Know your own variables
- Know the other party's variables
- Have pre-planned negotiation moves of low cost, high value variables
- Have pre-planned variables you want to ask for in return
- Knowledge of the client and their business
- Any historical agreements with the client or precedents which may have been set
- Any inside information on the particular individuals you will see.

Even if you have only done the above, you are so much more ready. This far exceeds the normal procedure of a five-minute chat in a cab on the way to the client where all you agree is who will lead the meeting. (You know you have done that!)

This level of preparation will transform how you feel and what you can achieve.

So let us now focus on the actual negotiation itself.

We will now explore a simple three-step guide on how to have a negotiation discussion – three easy steps to remember and three easy ways to know where you are in a negotiation.

Golden Rule No 9 – What is the gap?

Golden Rule No 10 – Trade the variables.

Golden Rule No 11 – Close the deal.

The best example I have of Golden Rule No. 9, "What is the Gap" is a tale of my embarrassing Dad!

Embarrassing Dad

EXAMPLE

You know when you are in your teenage years you begin to develop a bit of a complex about your parents? Well this situation took it to a whole new level!

I was 17, had passed my driving test, and had always been interested in cars and motorcycles – a passion which continues to this day. It was a Saturday and I was out with my father when I told him about a new car which had just been released. He suggested we go and have a look – just look!

There it was in the showroom, with its price emblazoned across the windscreen in big orange numbers.

A salesman came out and asked if he could help. Immediately, my father replied, *"How much is that car?"* I thought, *"Oh come on, Dad, it's right there on the windscreen."*

The salesman pointed to the car and said the price on the screen, to which my father replied, *"I can read! I mean how much is it really?"*

Somewhat taken aback, the salesman said, *"Well I'm sure we could do a wee bit better than that."*

"How much better?" Dad replied.

The salesman walked away into an office, came back out a minute later and gave a lower price.

"Is that your best price?" Dad asked.

"Yes that would be the best we could do," the salesman replied.

"Okay, thank you," Dad replied and we started to walk out. All of a sudden the salesman followed and asked if we could still be interested. Dad responded that at the price quoted, probably not.

"Well I am sure we could find a deal that would suit and we could talk about it," the salesman stated. This was when it started to become really embarrassing!

Dad said, *"Talk about what? I just asked if that was your best deal and you said yes. So, is it your best deal or not? I am here to potentially buy a car, not make a friend – is it your best deal or not?"*

The salesman started to walk over to the office he had gone to earlier and Dad said, *"Look, just go and bring the organ grinder out here!"*

Oh my word, I was astounded! I thought, how can you say that to the guy, insinuating he's the monkey? Do not worry, however, it gets worse!

The Sales Manager appeared from the office and took over proceedings. *"We could probably do another £xx off."*

Then the variables kicked in! In those days (as I am now advancing in years a little!) cars did not automatically come with passenger wing mirrors or passenger sun visors or headrests, radios, foot mats, or mud flaps and many other things. They were all extras unless you bought the top spec model.

So Dad said, *"The price sounds good and I take it that includes interior mats?"*

"No it doesn't, I'm afraid."

"Okay then," and Dad began to walk out!

"Okay, we'll put interior mats in it."

"And mud flaps," stated Dad.

"No."

"No? You mean you would let me walk out of here and not buy a car because you wouldn't put mud flaps on it?"

"Okay – mud flaps."

"And a full tank of fuel," Dad demanded.

"Okay."

Now this went on for a while with my father obviously running through a list in his head, with each demand causing me more embarrassment and discomfort. But nothing prepared me for what happened next . . . having made all of these demands and been given most of them, Dad said, *"I'll get back to you"* and we left!

After remonstrating about how embarrassing all that was, I then asked where we were going.

"To another dealership," he replied. I made it really clear I did not want to stand and go through that whole episode again and he

was rude! I was assured that same episode was not necessary and to just get in the car.

We went to the other dealership where Dad simply stated the deal he had been offered and inquired as to what they could offer.

"That's a good deal you have been offered," they said. *"I think we could match it."*

"I didn't drive over here for you to match it," Dad replied. *"I already have that deal – beat it!"*

After a little toing and froing they beat the deal – cue more embarrassment.

"Okay, I'll get back to you," Dad replied and we left!

"Where are we going now?" I asked.

"Back to the first garage!"

"No way, Dad, I am not going in there again," I said. But back we went and he dragged me in.

"We have been offered a better deal by another garage," and he told them what it was.

"Okay, we could probably match that."

"I didn't come back here for you to match it; I already have that deal – beat it!"

After another couple of frank exchanges, they beat the other deal and, totally surprising to me, Dad bought the car.

I was, however, still somewhat appalled by the whole episode and said as much when we left. Dad then took me for a cup of coffee as he wanted to explain something. We sat down and this is what he said:

"David, if we had bought the car for the price on the windscreen and nothing else, with no extras thrown in, the salesperson would not have gone home feeling guilty that he could have put so many extras on and didn't. This is business. If you don't ask you won't get. Anyway, it's the guy's fault because he never closed down the deal."

This last comment I never understood until I discovered the Golden Rules many years later, and I will explain soon.

So let's take this whole example and use it as the basis of explaining Golden Rules No. 9, 10, 11.

YOU   **OTHER PARTY (OP)**

When you are the seller, you know where you are, your terms of business, your fees etc. In your initial selling phase, these terms should have been presented. What you don't know is where they are as the buyer. What a good buyer will do is simply say that your terms and fees are unreasonable and ask you to start moving towards them.

YOU   **OTHER PARTY (OP)**

The problem is you have no idea at all as to how far you will have to move to secure agreement. If they simply keep saying no, and you keep moving towards them, who knows where you will end up – probably past where your walk-away point should have been.

The next step here is to ensure the other party puts a marker down as to where they are, and what they are seeking. You can say as the seller – "You say we are too expensive, so what wouldn't be?"

Never move until you know how far apart you are! If you feel like you must "do something" to break deadlock, offer a low cost, high value variable.

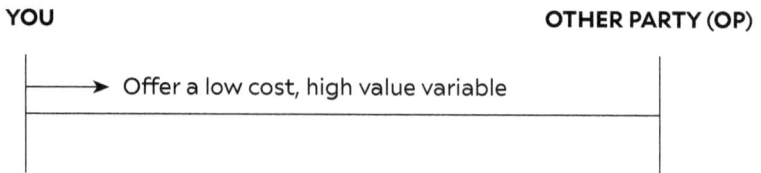

YOU   **OTHER PARTY (OP)**

→ Offer a low cost, high value variable

As the seller, you are asking the other party to put a marker down to show how far apart you are. If they are good, however, they will know that keeping you away from knowing where they are is key and they should simply say, *"Well, what's the best you can do? Not good enough!"*

The first step is to defend your position – sell! Talk about what it is the buyer will receive for the fees and defend your starting position. If you immediately start to move, there does not appear to be any pain, (Golden Rule no. 4) and that will only encourage the other party to keep asking for more.

Let me give a few examples from a buyer's perspective, which will help illustrate two things:

1. What to say and do when you are buying goods or services.
2. How to act when you are the seller in similar situations.

The 'No Hot Water' Hotel

I was doing a lot of work for a client in Edinburgh, Scotland. I always stayed in the same hotel and had been there numerous times.

On one of my visits I woke up in the morning to find there was no hot water in the bathroom, so was unable to wash/shower etc. I was leaving that day anyway and not staying for another night.

I phoned down to reception, told them of the problem, and they explained during the night one of the boilers had broken down and none of the rooms on my floor had hot water. They did, however, tell me to bring all my belongings downstairs and they would reallocate a room for me to wash and change in.

I packed all my things, put on my clothes from the previous day, and went to reception where I had to wait while some guests were checking out and others were similarly being reallocated rooms. I was given a new room key and trudged up to the room, to be pleasantly surprised that it was a beautiful suite. It would have been great had I been staying there, but all I was doing was washing, changing and leaving.

After getting ready I went back down to reception to check out and was presented with my bill. From memory it was £145 for bed & breakfast. Now here is where, as a buyer, it was not a time to make a specific demand, just ask the seller to move towards me.

I simply turned the bill around and asked, *"Can you please tell me where the hot water situation is reflected in the bill?"*

(Think for yourself right now, if this had been you with an original bill of £145, what would you have been willing to settle for? In my courses most people say about £100.)

The seller then simply said, *"I am very sorry, sir, would £50 be okay for your room?"*

Not £50 off, £50 total! I honestly would never have said I would only pay £50. I probably would have been happy at £100, but the key here as a buyer was not to make a specific demand and simply ask what is possible.

As the buyer, do not make specific demands. Just keep asking for a better deal or what else can be thrown in. You might be surprised at getting much more than you would have asked for.

EXAMPLE

The meal which went very wrong

I was out for dinner with my wife, a client and his wife. My client happened to have a passion for wine and had a deep knowledge of wines, regions, and what goes well with what food.

It was because of this I had chosen to take everyone to a new restaurant which had a considerable wine list.

Everything was going well, my client ordered a nice bottle of wine and it was brought to the table. Upon tasting the sample, my client looked at the waiter and said, *"I'm sorry but I think the wine is corked."*

The waiter sniffed the bottle and cork and said it was fine.

"No really, it is corked."

Astonishingly the waiter picked up a glass from a neighbouring table, poured some of the wine into it, took a sip and again said there was nothing wrong with it.

At this point I simply looked at the waiter with somewhat pleading eyes and asked please could it be changed for another bottle? Not a good start – but it got worse!

When our meals arrived, one of them was not very warm so we asked if that could be at least warmed up, if not replaced. The meal was taken away, leaving three of us eating at the insistence of the person who had no food. And then the replacement arrived, while three of us watched them eat! Not good at all!

This was supposed to have been an ideal place to treat a client, but unfortunately not. I left the table and walked up to the bar area where I asked to see the manager. The manager came, but there were other customers standing nearby so I asked if we could move over to the side.

(N.B. The reason I asked to move over to the side and a more private place was very simple. It is never a good idea to embarrass or humiliate someone in front of others. We are all only human and the reaction tends to be one of shutting down and the creation of a win/lose scenario. Always help people save face.)

In our more private space I explained about the wine, the meal, and how generally the whole evening had been unsatisfactory and how disappointed I was. No ranting, shouting or embarrassing people. I simply stated I was unhappy and asked what he could do about it.

The Manager was amazing. Having explained he thought our experience was unacceptable, and how sorry he was, he then pulled a masterstroke.

He took out his business card and, before offering me anything in recompense, he asked a brilliant question. *"Sir, would you give me your word that you would come back again, and I will guarantee you will not have a similar experience?"*

The reason I love this question was very simple. Golden Rule No. 8. Always trade, never give!

If I had said I would never darken his door again, he probably would have given me much less than he did. But he made sure we would come back before deciding what to do. I love it!

(Similar to the "No Hot Water Hotel", I want you to imagine being in this situation for yourself. If you were to make a specific demand (which we know you shouldn't as a buyer) what would you have been happy with? Take the wine and the meal off the bill? Free coffees and liqueurs?)

Well to my utter surprise the manager said, *"As for tonight, don't pay for anything!"*

I even started to apologise to him! I said he didn't need to do that, but he simply said that as long as I gave my word to come back, this evening was free.

My table was quite impressed I had negotiated everything for free; what a dream negotiator I must be! But there are two lessons in this story:

1. As a buyer, don't be specific and just ask what can be done. You might be surprised.
2. The manager still managed to save face and get a guarantee of a return visit.

Always trade, never give.

So, what do these examples demonstrate?

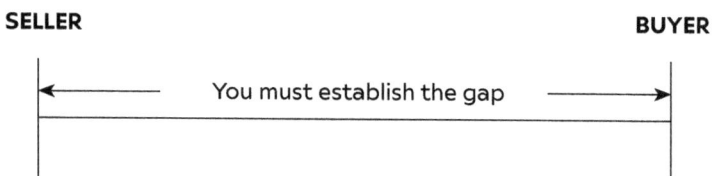

SELLER   **BUYER**

←———————— You must establish the gap ————————→

If you are the buyer, do not make specific demands. Simply tell the seller they need to keep coming towards you. If they cannot establish the gap, you are in a stronger position.

As a seller, you can now see how important it is to establish the gap before moving.

If you are told you are too expensive, ask what they would want.

If you are told your competitor is cheaper, ask what they are charging, and for what level of service.

Why do you think the first thing a car salesman asks is, *"What's your budget?"* They want to know where you are as a buyer and then they will probably attempt to move your budget up. Simply reply that your budget is flexible and you will know what you want when you see it. Spot the car you want and ask what the best deal would be and keep asking what else can be put on – at the last minute drop in the bombshell that it is over your budget and ask what they can do.

Remember my dad asking for lots of variables and basically saying "keep coming towards me"? It was years later after I learned and formulated the Golden Rules that I understood what he meant when he said to me that the seller did not close down the deal.

All the seller had to say to stop the incessant demands was, *"If I put mud flaps on the car will you buy it?"* Is there a deal to be done now or not? If Dad had replied that he was not sure, the seller could have said that if you commit to buy it now then I will put mud flaps on it. The deal would be closed at that point instead of all the demands after.

What happens, though, if the client makes some ridiculous demand? Let's say your terms are 25% and they say 8%. Because you know your walk-away point, you can have total confidence – "I am very sorry but at that fee I would be unable to take on the work. However, if and when you don't get what you are after, please come back to me as I would love to help."

However, if the buyer still wants to talk, we go to Golden Rule No. 10.

CHAPTER SUMMARY

1. As a buyer try to keep the seller away from knowing your position.

2. As a buyer try to not make specific demands. Simply ask the seller to keep moving towards you. You might be surprised what you receive.

3. As a seller, you must establish the gap. Do not move until you know where they are asking you to go.

4. If you are stuck, offer a low cost, high value variable to try to break the deadlock.

5. If the demands are way past your walk-away point, say so and assure the other party you want to help, the door is still open, and you are happy to help when circumstances change.

CHAPTER TEN

GOLDEN RULE NO· 10

"Trade the Variables"

"My father said; 'You must never try to make all the money that's in a deal. Let the other fellow make some money too, because if you have a reputation for always making all the money, you won't have many deals!'"

JEAN PAUL GETTY

So now you know how far apart you are, you can start working at bringing both parties together in a win/win fashion, about which everyone is happy.

This is only possible if you know the variables. If you do not know the variables, the coming together will be on the basis of discounting, not negotiating.

Three ways to narrow the gap

We have actually explored these already, but to reiterate:

1. "I can't do anything with the fee, but what I could maybe do is . . ." and offer a low cost, high value variable.
2. "I can do something with the fee, and what I would need from you is . . ." and ask for high value variables back.
3. A combination of the two above, preferably with your fee staying intact, offering low cost variables and gaining high value variables in return. "I can't do anything with the fee but what I maybe could do is . . . if we are able to agree for you to . . ."

Using our diagram yet again, let us assume the length of an arrow from your position is equivalent to the COST TO YOU of giving that variable: The shorter the arrow, the lower the cost of the variable.

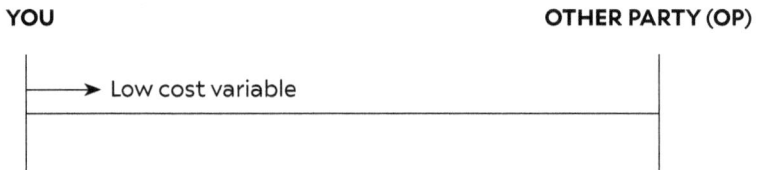

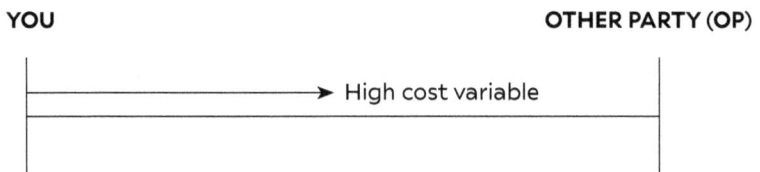

YOU   **OTHER PARTY (OP)**

→ Low cost variable

YOU   **OTHER PARTY (OP)**

→ High cost variable

If the low cost variable you offer is of HIGH VALUE to the OP, is their movement towards you the same length? No, they move dispropor-tionately towards you because of the value in receiving that variable.

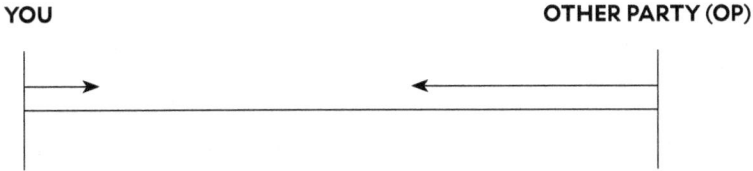

As such, you may be able to offer two low cost variables, which are of high value to the OP and they move much more towards you, striking that win/win deal everyone is happy with.

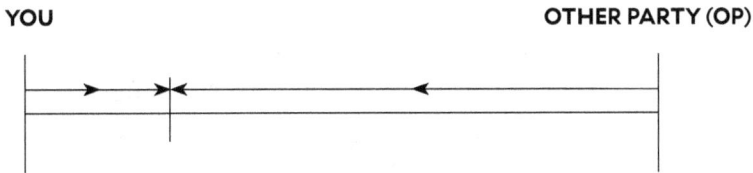

Beware of "Thank and Bank"

There is an old tactic trained buyers use called "Thank and Bank". This is where you need to be very specific about the exact words you use during this part of the discussion.

If you simply say, as your variable move, "I could give you an extended guarantee period", the likelihood is they will say, "Thank you, but I need more."

You have offered the variable and they have accepted it. They have "Thanked and Banked", you cannot take it back, and you will then be pressed to make another concession, upping your offer again. You are now a key variable down. They took it, banked it, and keep asking.

It is the same with any variable you offer straight out. You say they can have it, they will say thank you, put it in their proverbial top pocket and say you still need to do better, i.e. they will keep pressing for you to 'come over here' a bit more.

The key skill here is to "test offer" variables. Instead of saying:

"I could give you . . ." say, "I can't do anything with the fee but were I able to extend the guarantee period might that be of interest to you?"

Or

"How interested would you be if I were able to extend the guarantee period and minimise your risk?"

By adjusting exactly what you have said, you have not offered the variable or said they can have it. You have "test offered" it and it means they are unable to 'Thank and Bank' because you merely asked if it might be of interest.

Always 'test offer' your variables and always trade, never give. If you move, get something in return.

"I could possibly look at extending the guarantee period and handle the role myself if I was given exclusivity on it."

In addition an in-depth knowledge of the variables means you never have to turn down a deal again, no matter how bad it might first appear.

A belligerent bully of a buyer says: "Listen, do the work at 12% or get out!"

You could now reply very positively using the variables. "I think I might be able to do that. If you are able to give me a percentage of the fee upfront, exclusivity on the role, provide me with introductions to the rest of your business, a day of interview slots, access to all your temp recruitment, and one of my team handles the role instead of me we might be able to get there"

They might seriously balk at that reply, but there are three key things happening here:

1. You are not saying no to the OP. You are negotiating with them.
2. They are the one turning down the deal, not you.
3. They know you are not about to roll over and have your tummy tickled.

This keeps the negotiation alive and means you may be able to go on to ask: "So were I able to take my fee down (not necessarily to 12%) what could you do for me apart from give me this role?"

At the end of Golden Rule No 1 it was emphasized that people like to deal with experts and professionals who evidently know what they are doing. Be that professional, knowledgeable, expert. This is a place to show it!

I also made a bold promise in the preface of this book – "You are about to learn how to earn more for the work you do and amazingly even how to do the same work for the same fees and still go on to earn more."

Can you now see how that is possible?

1. Keep your fees more intact by offering low cost, high value variables instead.
2. If you do have to do the same work at the same fees as you did before, simply get more in return by asking for more variables back.

In the words of that ever so popular insurance advert – "Simples"!

CHAPTER SUMMARY

1. Always offer low cost, high value variables first.

2. The movement of the OP towards you is then disproportionate.

3. "I can't do anything with the fee but what I maybe could do is ..."

4. "I can do something with the fee and what I would need in return is ..."

5. "I can't do anything with the fee but what I maybe could do is ... if we are able to agree for you to ..."

6. Beware of 'Thank and Bank'.

7. Always <u>test offer</u> variables.

CHAPTER ELEVEN

GOLDEN RULE NO· 11

"Close the Deal"

*"Make sure you are absolutely clear about
what you have just agreed, because chances
are the other party isn't."*

———

AUTHOR

Now you both feel you have reached a satisfactory conclusion it is imperative to Close The Gap.

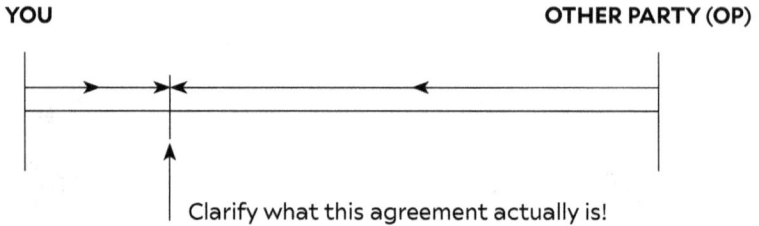

YOU   **OTHER PARTY (OP)**

Clarify what this agreement actually is!

Closing the gap simply means clarifying for both parties exactly what has been agreed.

The reasons for the necessity of this are simple:

1. Misunderstandings
2. Bad memories
3. Convenient differences

1. Misunderstandings

It is so easy for all concerned to lose track as to what exactly has just been agreed.

EXAMPLE

Strike a deal

On my two-day, more in-depth 12 Golden Rules programme for senior managers, all the delegates participate in a pre-written negotiation exercise where two teams negotiate with each other over a particular business deal.

The exercise is time bound and the teams are told some form of agreement has to be reached. Usually with about ten seconds to go, they strike a deal and all shake hands. Immediately I ask all members of both teams to write down their understanding of the deal they have just struck.

99% of the time two things occur:

1. The two teams do not agree with what the other team is saying the deal was.
2. Worse, even people within the same team don't agree what their own deal was!

They have just spent a long time getting to the point of agreement, have shaken hands on it and yet don't actually know what was agreed.

There is no subterfuge here at all, only misunderstandings. They simply did not close the gap.

2. Memory Loss

When work on a particular assignment will occur over a few weeks or months, it is very easy for all parties concerned to genuinely forget what was agreed. Again, no ill will or trying to make things difficult, just an inability to remember exactly what was said so long ago. The reason? No proper closing of the gap.

3. Convenient Differences

Some rather less scrupulous individuals, however, will use one or both of the above challenges to "conveniently forget or misunderstand". As we explored in Golden Rule No 7, if you have done the work, the candidate is placed and then these issues arise, you have lost your negotiation leverage. They know this.

"I never agreed to that, what I meant was . . ."

"Oh I think we have a problem, I thought you meant . . ."

If the gap has not been closed properly, there is room for that unscrupulous individual to manoeuvre, wriggle and make things difficult. Room even to make you doubt what you said at the time, with little room to negotiate because the client has already received what they wanted.

So how do you close the gap?

1. Discuss the exact deal while still in the meeting.
2. Follow up in writing.

1. Verbally summarizing everything in the meeting

In the meeting, when all seems to have been agreed, it is essential there is a verbal summary of exactly what is going to happen. This often does not occur, however, because people do not like talking about money.

- The elegant way of summarizing the agreement is to talk about all the things you are going to do for the OP **FIRST**. What you are going to do in the assignment, including all those variables you normally never mention which are already included in your service, plus the additional ones you have agreed to.
- Only then talk about what the OP has agreed to and the fees they will pay.

The reason for always putting your concessions and service first is so the OP obtains full visibility of all you will do, have given, and what they will receive. This way, when it comes to what they have agreed to, they have context and can give themselves the comfort of the concessions they gave and that the fees they are paying are worth it.

2. *Follow Up In Writing*

This is a very simple principle which is often overlooked. Busy peo-ple, wanting to get started on the assignment, may find this part tedious or even unnecessary, but it is absolutely essential. Having had the discussion in the meeting, it is vital to have some form of written record of the agreement just made.

The best way to do this is obvious – have a signed contract; signed terms of business. That is the belt and braces way of ensuring every-thing is clear and by far the safest way to go. It can throw up a few challenges though:

1. Contracts usually have to be run past legal teams in companies to ensure they are not unreasonable, and believe me, to jus-tify their existence, lawyers <u>always</u> find something they think is unreasonable.
2. As a result of point 1 they tend to slow everything down. If it is a large contract, that delay can be worth it. Often, however, what you are dealing with is not worthy of that level of detail.

I am not suggesting you try to avoid contracts. That would be fool-ish. But in the absence of contracts there are other ways to close the gap in writing which still work – email, letter, etc

- When writing the agreement down, do it the same way as in the meeting, first talking about all you will do, and have given. For the same reasons as above.
- You also have two options at this point – two ways you can write the email or letter:

1. Opt in letters
2. Opt out letters

1. Opt in:

This is where you would write everything down and request from the OP that they confirm they are happy i.e. they have to opt in to the agreement. An example would be where you finish with: "Please would you confirm you are happy with the above and I will then proceed".

The challenge is that often you will wait to hear back because people are bombarded by so much correspondence and email these days.

2. Opt out:

This is where you write everything down, but instead of asking the OP to confirm back that they are happy, you ask them to come back to you only if they are not happy. An example of this would be:

> "I am assuming all of the above is an accurate summary of what we discussed and agreed, and I will proceed on this basis unless you tell me otherwise".

The OP now does not have to do anything if they are happy, and it also helps you as you can simply crack on with the work. I would tend to recommend opt out as the normal way to go.

Legally however there is a timeframe within which opt out would be seen as reasonable. For example, the OP might be away on holiday for two weeks, not be able to respond, and therefore be in a position to query upon their return the validity of you pressing on without time to reply. However, in general, if they were around and did not choose to get back to you within two to three weeks, it would be reasonable for you to have proceeded on the understanding that everything was okay.

Here's a couple of other little nuggets. Nowadays pretty much everything is done via email, and don't we all know it! There are tons of it every day. If you really want to grab someone's attention, try some of these little tips:

1. Write them a letter. We receive fewer and fewer hard copies of things nowadays, so again it attracts attention.
2. Mark your emails to them "<u>Low Priority</u>" with the green exclamation mark. Everyone tends to mark everything urgent with the red exclamation and the green mark is so unusual and rare, people tend to open it!

Where I didn't close the gap

At one time when Whitewater was exceptionally busy, and myself in particular, I lost sight of the very principles I train upon in closing the gap. With three separate clients, I left client meetings, and due to being so busy and travelling so much I did not follow up in writing with a proper description of what we had agreed. I simply did not close the gap. The result was three separate assignments falling into completely unnecessary confusion and having to work twice as hard to bring the clients back on side. My fault. You have to close the gap.

Example – Where I did close the gap – thankfully!

There may be times you feel like you have a challenging/rubbish job but allow me to offer you some hope. Whilst at Procter & Gamble I was the Sales Marketing Manager for a number of Brands in the UK and Ireland, one of which was Old Spice! That was a challenging job!

Whilst I was a National Account Manager I was responsible for selling Old Spice, amongst other brands, to a well-known national toiletries retailer. This retailer had a reputation for "playing hard ball" and being heavily focused on undercutting its competition.

EXAMPLE

I received a phone call from my buyer late one Friday afternoon, which potentially could have ruined my life. I was informed that according to the customer I had been overcharging on Old Spice for almost a year and they wanted £725,000 returned to them. £725,000 is a big mistake to make, and I could see my career flashing past my eyes.

However, I was convinced this was a mistake by the customer. P&G's training is exceptional and all National Account Managers are trained to run their accounts in a similar way, being given key skills to employ – two of which are communication and filing.

I knew that Old Spice had gone up in price some time ago and I also knew I had definitely had that discussion with the buyer, but did I have it in writing?

In those days (I am unsure what happens now) for all key customer communications on things such as range changes, price changes and the like, we were trained to do five things:

1. Have a meeting with the customer to talk them through what was happening.
2. Compose a letter confirming the details and photocopy it.
3. Take the original letter and post it to them.
4. Take the photocopy of the letter to the fax machine and fax it to them, taking the fax confirmation sheet the machine produces and stapling it to the photocopy for filing.
5. Also write an email attaching a soft copy of the letter.

So apart from putting the Good Year blimp above their offices as well as a van with neon signs on it passing by, we could pretty much prove we had made every effort to inform the customer and had given plenty of notice.

The question was had I done that, and could I prove it? The training on filing now came into its own. I knew where to go to look.

If I had done what I was supposed to, it would be in a particular place – and it was – all of it!

I sent all of the correspondence back to the customer showing there had been a price rise and I had given plenty of notice it was to occur. I had properly closed the gap.

The customer accepted it was their error and my career was safe!

CHAPTER SUMMARY

1. Make sure everyone knows what has been agreed.

2. People misunderstand, forget, or conveniently differ.

3. Verbally summarize what has been agreed in the meeting.

4. Always outline what you are going to be doing for the other party before what they are doing in return.

5. Follow up in writing.

6. Signed contracts and terms of business are the best.

7. Failing the above, email, letter, etc

8. Write the agreement in the same way you talk it. Your concessions first.

9. Opt in is where you are asking them to get back to you with permission to proceed.

10. Opt out is where you ask the other party to respond only if they are unhappy.

CHAPTER TWELVE

GOLDEN RULE NO· 12

"You must adapt your style"

"It is not the strongest of the species that survives, nor the most intelligent, but the one most responsive to change."

—————————

CHARLES DARWIN

The final Golden Rule is simple – you *cannot* negotiate the same way every time. You need to adapt your own personal style to suit the situation in order to gain the best results.

There are many great tools out there to self-analyse your preferred negotiation style. The internet is full of them. They largely look at how collaborative you naturally are versus how competitive. To put it another way, how important having a good relationship is to you versus how important getting the deal is.

As per the rest of this book I want to keep it simple and easy to understand, so I am going to break negotiation styles down into four instantly recognizable chunks, which will allow you to self-assess, work on your strengths and also see ways to become even better. In this way it is easier to learn how to adapt your own preferred style to the differing scenarios you may face and be most effective ongoing.

Mr/Mrs Friendly		**Mr/Mrs Bully**	
	Feelings		Fights
FRIENDSHIP		FORCE	Winning
	Friends		
	Logic		
FACTS		FROLICS	"Doing a
	Data		Deal"
Mr/Mrs Logic		**Mr/Mrs Deal Doer (Del Boy!)**	

Let's take each in turn, look at the positives they bring, the pitfalls they may hide, the ways to maximize their effectiveness, and how they impact upon each other.

Mr/Mrs Friendly – "Friendship"

The predominant part of this style is genuine concern for having a good, positive relationship with the other party – a relationship which is friendly, understanding, and easy to deal with.

Recruitment tends to attract people who are interested in interpersonal relationships and who gain a lot personally from fostering them. However, they may find it very difficult to deal with others for whom relationships are not important, or not as important.

Positives of this style

- Trusting
- Sincere
- Approachable
- Relaxed
- Concerned
- Empathetic
- Honest
- Good listener
- People person
- Helpful

Great – a person genuinely caring about having a positive, friendly relationship and being a great relationship builder. However, they can be perceived as:

- A soft touch
- Someone who waffles
- Too eager to please
- Incapable of recognizing the real issues
- An over-promiser and under-deliverer
- An easy touch
- A capitulator
- Needing to be liked

'Friendly' can often believe that by giving in, they will go on to build a better relationship going forward. 'Friendly' is also how you might imagine most people would like to work. Unfortunately, it is not always like that. In fact, I would go so far as to say it is becoming less usual nowadays for this to be the case. As we have said before, companies are having to focus strongly on costs and this often can be at the expense of building cosy relationships with suppliers.

Beware of the Gimp!

Indeed, it is to counteract the existence and development of these relationships that many larger organizations have gone for what I affectionately refer to as "the Gimp approach". I may be somewhat unfair here but please allow me some dramatic licence. Apologies to my fellow professionals painted in the following light.

"The Gimp" is the person who appears in a negotiation out of nowhere and usually comes from "the Procurement Department".

In my mind's eye they have been kept in the dark, in the basement of the building for many days, with little or nothing to eat, and are then told there is a supplier upstairs! They are let out and come into the meeting with a fury, demanding all and sundry, and taking no prisoners whatsoever. Are they interested in relationships? Not even slightly. Their job is to drive costs down. Here is a question – when the gimp tells you they only work at 15% and nothing more, are they negotiating with you, or are they "selling" you their own deal? They are selling you! Selling is more powerful than negotiating – that's why you should stop negotiating and sell better – Golden Rule No 1.

So what happens then when Mr/Mrs Friendly meets the Gimp? The ill-prepared 'Friendly' loses almost every time – eaten alive!

Having a friendly, trusting, empathetic, relaxed approach is not wrong at all as long as it can be backed up with strength and prepa-ration. As we shall see, being an unreasonable, belligerent bully does not get you everywhere either.

How can you improve if this is your style?

1. Recognise not everyone wants to be your friend and that is ok.
2. This is not personal, it is business, and everyone is probably encountering the same resistance from the OP concerned.
3. The key ways to gain better results are to prepare, and disassociate yourself from the situation.
4. Trying to please the OP can erode your standing and your margin.

Mr/Mrs Bully – "Winning"

The predominant part of this style is an absolutist approach to getting what they want. It is my way or no way. In rugby, there is an expression whimsically called the "Maori sidestep" which comes from the New Zealand All Blacks, the most successful international rugby team in history. (NB they are also the most successful team of any team sport in history!) A sidestep by definition is where a player makes a physical movement that puts the opponent off-balance, enabling the player to run around or past them. The Maori sidestep, however, is not a sidestep at all – it involves making no attempt to go around anyone, but rather, straight over the top of them! This can be the driving philosophy of the 'Bully' style.

What this style is interested in is <u>winning.</u>

Positives of this style

- Confident
- Charismatic
- Strong
- Competitive
- Leads from the front

- Determined
- Committed
- Keen to achieve
- Let's you know where you stand

Great – a strong and determined style which does not fall over easily and will be willing to stand firm. Sounds fantastic, and maybe even the best. However, they can be perceived as:

- Stubborn
- A bully
- Aggressive
- A short fuse
- Having tunnel vision
- Being unwilling to find better solutions
- "Leading with the chin" in boxing parlance
- Inflexible

How can you improve if this is your style?

1. If this is your preferred style it may well work most of the time. Unfortunately, it is probably not a methodology for gaining long-term business. Individuals eventually become tired of such reckless and one-sided behaviour, even if it is done with a smile on your face and a dagger in your hand!
2. More importantly, always having to win can, over time, erode the longer term partnerships which may have served you well.
3. Be reasonable.
4. Look for other ways to gain what you want rather than steam-rollering the OP. "There is more than one way to skin a cat."

Mr/Mrs Logic – Sense

The way you negotiate could well be based on logic, facts and data. You may not be easily swayed by either friendly or bully behaviour and rather focus on the facts of the situation in trying to achieve agreement.

Positives of this style

- Analytical
- Cool
- Calm
- Collected

- Calculated
- Thorough
- Evaluative

- Prepared
- Attention to detail

Great – a calm individual who has prepared and can work the detail. Sounds fantastic. However, they can be perceived as:

- Cold
- Dull
- Emotionally blocked
- Not creative
- Having "Analysis Paralysis"
- Being unable to adapt
- Not recognizing the value of dedication and commitment
- Always sticking to the script
- Inflexible

Preferring to negotiate like this is an incredible talent because it actually depends on some work! 'Friendly' and 'Bully' behaviour are dependent on an emotional response, which comes fairly naturally, but preparation here is key and can be a great strength.

Not all deals, though, are done purely from rational, fact-based detail and for some, there is no need to venture down this route at all.

I once came across an example where a massive corporation really wanted to buy a family-run business which had long-standing expertise in a particular niche market and product line. The corporation could take the product global, but the family business also had other offers. The corporation lost out to another company in the purchase for a very simple reason. The successful purchaser recognized the value to the family of having the family name still associated with the product. The logic-driven corporation would not even acknowledge the name was an important piece of the puzzle and kept saying it had no value in the wider world. The corporation was actually correct – the name did not have value in the wider world, but they failed to realize and accept just how important the continuation of a family name would be to the family itself. That was a very high value variable to them, albeit an emotional one.

How can you improve if this is your style?

1. Everything is not rational! Behaviour is not always based on cold hard facts. Sometimes you have to allow others to have their personal feelings taken into account.
2. Prepare for multiple scenarios, not just one. The need to go away and re-evaluate can slow things down too much, so a more flexible approach could serve you well.
3. Prepare on the basis of the variables. What are the low cost, high value trades you can do early? This is the easiest to improve.
4. Have someone with you who is better at relationships and deal making.

Mr/Mrs Deal Doer – "Dealing"

What drives this last style is the whole act of making deals. They love the dynamic nature of striking a deal and thrive on the "ducking and diving" nature of it all. Doing a deal is paramount in their mind, with little heed being paid to feelings, facts or fights! Think of the television character already mentioned in this book, Del Boy from *Only Fools and Horses* and you will have a good idea of this style.

Positives of this style

- Think on their feet
- Sociable
- Flexible
- Imaginative
- Opportunistic
- Likeable
- Creative
- Entrepreneurial
- Can always find a way
- Looks for alternative routes

Great – someone who is out there making things happen, finding new ways to do that, and clinching new business. However, they can be perceived as:

- Insincere
- Disorganized
- A person who over-promises and under-delivers
- Too clever
- Moving too quickly
- Only having a short-term view
- Not inspiring confidence
- Someone who can "outwit" the other party
- Flaky

Being a "deal doer" is a real skill. To be that flexible, dynamic and creative is a powerful talent. It can enable achieving agreements even with "Bully" or "Logic" due to the innate ability of seeing new opportunities and ways to get there. I have seen these types of individuals create and make up brand new variables, which didn't even exist before, in a meeting – on the spot!

The watch-outs here are simple. You can come across as somewhat of a dodgy individual! The ability to think and move quickly can be off-putting to those who are unable to do so, leading to a feeling that somewhere in proceedings you are winning and they cannot see where. This feeling can lead to the other party shutting down, fearful of agreement in case they are being outwitted and thus refusing to move forward.

How can you improve if this is your preferred style?

1. Slow down a little.
2. Show how what you are suggesting works for the other party.
3. Make sure you can deliver what you are about to promise.
4. Beware of creating deals which set a long term precedent and can come back to bite you and your business in the longer term.

What is your profile?

We all naturally have a certain amount of each style. There are, however, ways we simply prefer to work. The great news is that preferences are not necessarily binding. The fact that we have preferences in no way means we are unable to develop the other styles or learn how to enhance our skills in other areas.

If the four styles together need to equal 100% and we can assign a certain percentage value to each for our own ways of working, it can instantaneously show where we may need to develop.

Let me give you my own personal example below. Before learning the Twelve Golden Rules my profile would have looked like the following:

Mr/Mrs Friendly		Mr/Mrs Bully	
	Feelings		Fights
FRIENDSHIP		FORCE	Winning
	Friends		
65%		**5%**	
	Logic		
FACTS		FROLICS	"Doing a Deal"
	Data		
Mr/Mrs Logic		**Mr/Mrs Deal Doer (Del Boy!)**	
5%		**25%**	

The key driver for me was "Friendly", and still is! The next key strength was "Deal Doer". I loved finding ways to achieve deals being done, was good at working off the cuff, and gained a thrill from closing.

Unfortunately, when confronted by a bully the need to please kicked in. Why do they not like me? Why do they have to be so unreasonable? Can't they see I am trying to be easy to work with?

Furthermore, my ability to work creatively and on the move meant I tended not to prepare well enough. As a result, when I met a "Logic" I would be confronted by a lot of preparation and someone else who did not want to be my friend. They knew more than me, were more ready for the discussion and came armed with data for which I often struggled to find an answer.

The great thing about learning the Twelve Golden Rules, and being able to see my own profile so clearly, was I knew where I could improve. I needed to be stronger and less relationship driven and also needed to be better prepared. Indeed, the enhanced strength could easily be gained simply by better preparation; knowing the variables, having a walk-away point, being able to chunk up and so on.

By realizing this I was still able to be friendly and dynamic, but with the added strength not to be railroaded as well as being far better prepared.

So what is your profile?

Take the empty table below and put your personal scores in the boxes.

Mr/Mrs Friendly	Mr/Mrs Bully
Feelings FRIENDSHIP Friends ? ___%	Fights FORCE Winning ? ___%
Logic FACTS Data Mr/Mrs Logic ? ___%	FROLICS "Doing a Deal" Mr/Mrs Deal Doer (Del Boy!) ? ___%

What are your scores telling you? What are your key strengths to keep and develop? Where are the areas to improve?

Compatibility

At the risk of appearing to be writing a book similar to Astrology and Star Signs, the last pointers here are concerning the compatibility between differing approaches; when X meets Y and what to do. We will take each style, look at how it works with the others, and some easy ways to recognise how to cope and potentially gain better results ongoing. This is not supposed to be the definitive long-winded handbook, but merely a guide that may prove useful.

If you are Friendly and you meet . . .

1.   When Friendly meets Friendly

This can seem to be utopia – two really friendly people enjoying working together and happy in each other's company. The watch-out here is never actually getting to any agreement and solely booking another meeting to discuss it further! There needs to be a way of pushing ever so slightly to gain a fixed understanding and a clear set of parameters to move forward. Still stay friendly and simply state:

"I suppose we need to actually agree what we are doing here . . ."

2.   When Friendly Meets Bully

Big Trouble! The chances are the Bully will completely overwhelm an ill-prepared relationship builder and there is rarely an unusual outcome here. The temptation can be to capitulate in the hope of a better relationship further on. You need to be better prepared and be willing to stand your ground.

Here is a friendly way of stopping the potential wave of force being placed upon you – be disarmingly friendly. Say, for example:

"Have I done something personally to offend or upset you?"

This can often take the wind out of their sails a little and prompt a temporary halt in aggression, which may then be used to good advantage going forward. In addition, whilst it may seem odd from a Friendly perspective, Bully can often be impressed and indeed somewhat comforted by seeing your unwillingness to simply give in to their demands without so much as a discussion. They can see it as reassuring that you are willing to stand your ground, as it signals they are dealing with a professional who values their own service.

3. When Friendly Meets Logic

Any ill prepared person (not just Friendly) will struggle here. Friendly can become upset by the apparent absence of any emotion, see the other party as a dull individual, and not really want to do business with them. The key is to have prepared yourself. Know the variables, know any previous precedents which have been set, be ready to sell hard and show pain. You can use disarming friendliness again here too by simply smiling and reiterating:

> "I am very keen to find a way which suits us both. Let me dig a little deeper into the details for us both and see what we can achieve together."

If they are being unreasonable, use the prisoner's dilemma.

4. When Friendly meets Deal Doer

Beware! This slick talking, agreeable individual may be able to outwit, outflank, and out-manoeuvre you and they often do. You might not even have seen it either! Slow them down. Ask for more detail and set very clear parameters and timescales, which they must honour:

> "So if I understand what you are saying, we are agreeing to . . ."

If you are Bully and you meet . . .

1. When Bully meets Friendly

The chances are you are going to gain what you want. Being able to state clearly what you are after and demand it openly will usually work. However, bear in mind that ultimately the other party may not be giving you what you *could have* achieved because they are fed up with being put in a very difficult and overwhelming situation.

A calming phrase to Friendly can be:

> "I am in no way wanting to put you personally in a difficult position. This is simply what I need from a business perspective."

2. When Bully meets Bully

This could be trouble and mean war! You could also lose out. The temptation here is to lock horns and make it a win/lose fight to the death, which achieves nothing. Agreement can be difficult to reach as each party becomes too focused on the notion of beating the other person, losing creativity and becoming entrenched in their own position.

The key here can be to use your strength to robustly put forward friendly and logical solutions as well as being somewhat creative in the proposals you have prepared in advance. Simply falling back to an aggressive position and being unwilling to move can eliminate the opportunities to chunk up, find better ways, and gain the sort of ongoing agreements which would work in your favour.

3. When Bully meets Logic

Interesting one. There is a very good chance your tactic of simply steamrollering people will not work here with Logic, for two reasons:

- They tend not to react to emotional situations in the same way, or the retreating way you may have hoped for.
- They can dismantle proposals by dissecting the detail and offering up their own suggestions, which are based on data rather than outlandish emotional blackmail.

You need to be better prepared in order to make logical counter offers and proposals which they must then evaluate.

4. When Bully meets Deal Doer

Another interesting one. There are a few scenarios which can emerge here. Deal Doer may well simply agree, take the business and move on, fairly unscathed by Bully's tactics, and more than happy to have won the business. Another can be that Bully is too slow to react and Deal Doer is successfully pushing outcomes through which, if Bully had stopped to analyse them, could actually be sub-optimal.

Slow it down, look for the moves and be analytically critical.

If you are Logic and you meet . . .

1. When Logic meets Friendly

We know you are well prepared and we know there are numbers that make sense. In general a well prepared, well thought out and reasonable proposal will prevail. Particularly if Friendly's skills run out after simply being friendly.

If you really want to develop any form of ongoing relationship with Friendly however, there needs to be an ability to recognize the signs where emotion is playing a part. Are they chasing targets? Do they have good reasons and pressures heavily influencing them which if you could recognize and help with they would be a valuable ally ongoing? If you can help in these areas you will most probably end up with not only what you want, but more than you expected.

2. *When Logic Meets Bully*

Your preparation here is key. You tend not to be overly swayed by heavy emotional pressure so you are in a good position to do well. Use your logical approach to potentially undermine the force from the other party and stay calm. Be aware of the work done before, agreed rates, and the prisoner's dilemma.

A key tactic here can be to make sure Bully gains some concession or other, so they have the satisfaction they have done their job properly and gained something more. They will not be happy or think it is win/win if they have simply agreed to what you are initially proposing. Use low cost, high value variables to do this.

3. *When Logic meets Logic*

Now this can either be rather refreshing or somewhat of a struggle. If all the numbers add up, the proposals are rationally based and make sense to both parties, it can be quite easy to agree. There can be a tendency to end up trying to "out-logic" the other party though, which can lead to paralysis in the negotiations.

This is not a competition as to who has the most numbers or the best prepared scenarios. Focus on gaining a good outcome regardless of who looks best at the end. In addition, not every single agreement has to be gone through with a fine toothcomb. Unless it is a huge contract which needs this sort of scrutiny, allow more flexibility, and develop the skill of quickly assessing the rationale of the OP proposals.

4. When Logic meets Deal Doer

Where you can possibly struggle here is that you are going to encounter someone who wants to work quickly and move on. They will likely be able to put a number of options to you, many of which will have been impossible for you to prepare, so the ability for you to do two things will be key. Either:

- Slow the OP down so you can clearly see what is being proposed and stick with your well-reasoned arguments; or
- Speed up yourself, and allow yourself the freedom to assess proposals more quickly as they arise, rather than having to go away again and look at them more closely.

If you are Deal Doer and you meet . . .

1. When Deal Doer meets Friendly

The chances are you are going to get your own way here. Your personable style appeals to Friendly and you should use that. There can be a couple of temptations here:

- Steamroller them, do the deal and run, potentially leaving them in a poor position ongoing which can come back to you later on.
- You may frighten them! The pace and energy you bring can be off-putting, convincing them they are being in some way "bamboozled" by you, which can lead to them shutting down and not being willing to deal with you at all.

Slow down, be fair, make agreements which are win/win, preserve their own personal reputation, and ensure you are bringing them with you.

2. *When Deal Doer meets Bully*

You can do well here. Your entrepreneurial spirit and capability may enable you to duck and swerve the onslaught from Bully, ultimately enabling you to do a deal where others have failed. Watch-outs are:

- Simply agreeing with Bully as you can see there is a deal to be done regardless of its quality, and therefore setting a poor ongoing precedent for the rest of the business or those who will follow on from you looking after this client.
- Agreeing too quickly and promising things that in the cold light of day are very difficult to deliver. Even in the short term this can cause problems with the client due to disappointment, and they will never be shy in letting you know just how disappointed they are, and how unwilling they may now be to pay the bill!

Use your skill to "weather the storm" of Bully. Never see this as just a one-off situation as they will come back to you over and over again should they be unhappy. Make sure you can deliver what you are agreeing and consider the precedents you may be setting. Prepare more. Know your variables so you are trading, never giving.

3. *When Deal Doer Meets Logic*

These are not generally the people you like to do business with. They can appear slow, methodical and taking up too much of your time. You can become frustrated by the fact that much of what you suggest either has to be taken away for further analysis, or is slowly dissected in front of you.

Be patient, and better prepared. What you are trying to achieve is a business agreement, not make a new friend to go to the pub with. They need the detail and you must be able to provide it for them to feel comfortable. Yet again your speed can come across as being somewhat disconcerting, worrying Logic they are missing something and encouraging them to leave the negotiation for further thought.

Your ability to think on your feet can help Logic though. They probably have never thought of some of the approaches you are proposing and it can give them new ways of working they have never considered.

Make sure you have the detail or you will either be undermined, or mistrusted.

4. *When Deal Doer meets Deal Doer*

Now you are happy. The chances are, everything will happen very quickly and you will end up in the pub together. Do the deal, ensuring it is actually worthy, sets no ongoing precedents, and enjoy their company!

CHAPTER SUMMARY

1.   Those who can adapt more, can achieve more.

2.   You cannot negotiate the same way with everyone.

3.   Look at your preferred style(s) and use the strengths they bring.

4.   Look at your less preferred styles and work on them.

SUMMARY AND
FINAL THOUGHTS

Before giving you a summary of the Golden Rules for your ease and convenience I wanted to add some final thoughts.

Firstly – these skills work! I have personally trained thousands of recruiters on the Golden Rules and those who have chosen to implement have benefited from them massively.

Secondly – there is no "silver bullet". You may come up against genuinely unreasonable people in your time and there is no getting past them. That does not mean the skills do not work the vast majority of the time.

Thirdly – these skills take practice. I have been told numerous times by people who attended my trainings they "tried the skills once" and they didn't work – so they stopped! This is a disaster. Keep going. Keep using them. They pay off and it might take a while for you to get used to using them but that dedication will be worth it in the end.

Fourthly – you can do this! You personally have the capability to learn, practise, internalise and use these skills every day for the rest of your career. Commit to getting better at them and as you see your success grow be thankful you did.

Lastly – as you start to gain the results from these skills you are going to come under attack! From your own colleagues! They will start to believe you always get the good clients and that you are lucky. You won't be lucky, you will be smart! And good for you!

I wish you every good fortune for a happy, healthy and definitely more prosperous career.

THE TWELVE GOLDEN RULES

GOLDEN RULE NO· 1

"Stop negotiating and sell better"

1. There is a difference between selling and negotiation.
2. There is a point where one stops and the other starts.
3. People like to deal with experts and professionals who evidently know what they are doing. Be that professional, knowledgeable expert.
4. Good sellers negotiate less because they don't have to.
5. The only person capable of showing the other party the value of yourself and your service is you.
6. If you believe that you *have* to negotiate – you will always negotiate.

GOLDEN RULE NO· 2

"It's about belief systems and comfort levels"

1. Belief systems and comfort levels drive negotiation.
2. You can negotiate on almost everything.
3. It is going to happen to you consistently for the rest of your career.
4. Get comfortable and learn how to deal with it.

GOLDEN RULE NO· 3

"A good deal is in your head"

1. Always strive for a win/win.
2. Win/win is *anywhere* both parties are happy.
3. Win/win moves around based on circumstances.
4. Win/win is a *feeling* not a point.

GOLDEN RULE NO· 4

"It has to look like it hurts""

1. You have to know when to walk out, before you walk in.
2. A predetermined walk-away point gives you confidence.
3. A walk-away point by nature means the closer you get to it, the more pain you show.
4. Going in low, and trying to then negotiate up never works.
5. Talk money not percentages
6. Move in smaller increments towards your walk-away point.
7. Move in decreasing sized increments towards your walk-away point
8. Use a very specific odd number

GOLDEN RULE NO· 5

"You have to know when to walk out before you walk in"

1. You have to know when to walk out, before you walk in.
2. A predetermined walk-away point gives you confidence.
3. A walk-away point by nature means the closer you get to it, the more pain you show.
4. Again, going in low, and trying to then negotiate up never works.
5. Move in smaller increments towards your walk away point. Move in decreasing sized increments towards your walk-away point

GOLDEN RULE NO· 6

"When stuck, chunk up"

1. When stuck, chunk up!
2. Focus on common goals, not starting positions.
3. Use the Prisoner's Dilemma.
4. If the demands are past your walk-away point – walk away.
5. If you *have* to move, make the OP work for it – it will feel better to them.

GOLDEN RULE NO· 7

"You MUST know the variables"

1. You are always negotiating with what things are worth, not what they cost.
2. There are many things you have to negotiate with, other than price.
3. There are many things you could gain in return as well as the work.
4. Learn the variables, both yours and theirs.

GOLDEN RULE NO· 8

"Always trade never give"

1. If the fee changes the deal must change.
2. You do not simply give concessions without asking for something in return.
3. There are many ways to trade in situations that seem impassable.
4. You can only successfully trade if you know the variables.
5. "I can't do anything with the fee, but what I possibly could do is . . ." (offer low cost, high value variables).
6. "I could do something with the fee, and what I would need from you is . . ." (ask for variables back).

GOLDEN RULE NO· 9

"What is the gap?"

1. As a buyer try to keep the seller away from knowing your position.
2. As a buyer try to not make specific demands. Simply ask the seller to keep moving towards you. You might be surprised what you receive.
3. As a seller, you must establish the gap. Do not move until you know where they are asking you to go.
4. If you are stuck, offer a low cost, high value variable to try to break the deadlock.
5. If the demands are way past your walk-away point, say so and assure the other party you want to help, the door is still open, and you are happy to help when circumstances change.

GOLDEN RULE NO· 10

"Trade the variables"

1. Always offer low cost, high value variables first.
2. The movement of the OP towards you is then disproportionate.
3. "I can't do anything with the fee but what I maybe could do is . . ."
4. "I can do something with the fee and what I would need in return is . . ."
5. "I can't do anything with the fee but what I maybe could do is . . . if we are able to agree for you to . . ."
6. Beware of 'Thank and Bank'.
7. Always <u>test offer</u> variables.

GOLDEN RULE NO· 11

"Close the deal"

1. Make sure everyone knows what has been agreed.
2. People misunderstand, forget, or conveniently differ.
3. Verbally summarize what has been agreed in the meeting.
4. Always outline what you are going to be doing for the other party before what they are doing in return.
5. Follow up in writing.
6. Signed contracts and terms of business are the best.
7. Failing the above, email, letter, etc
8. Write the agreement in the same way you talk it. Your concessions first.
9. Opt in is where you are asking them to get back to you with permission to proceed.
10. Opt out is where you ask the other party to respond only if they are unhappy.

GOLDEN RULE NO· 12

"You MUST adapt your style"

1. Those who can adapt more, can achieve more.
2. You cannot negotiate the same way with everyone.
3. Look at your preferred style(s) and use the strengths they bring.
4. Look at your less preferred styles and work on them.

- The only thing better than this book is coming on the training course.

- Join the thousands of recruiters who have been trained in person.

- Have you and your business trained live.

- Learn the 12 Golden Rules

    + BONUS - Learn the 10 most common buyer tactics and EXCATLY what to say back to them.

    + BONUS - Have a live Q&A with David himself.

For more information about how you can have David personally train you and your team either live or online please contact

hello@maclemons.com

www.ingramcontent.com/pod-product-compliance
Lightning Source LLC
Chambersburg PA
CBHW071851200326
41519CB00016B/4335